AI Spatial Intelligence Explained

Jon Adams
Alex Rossi

CONTENTS

INTRODUCTION

Welcome to "AI Spatial Intelligence Explained," an exploration of the burgeoning world where artificial intelligence meets spatial reasoning, visualization, and problem-solving. This book delves into the intricate dance between spatial intelligence and AI, showcasing how these disciplines intersect to drive innovation in robotics, computer vision, and autonomous systems. Through rigorous yet accessible analysis, coupled with real-world examples and practical applications, this book aims to unfold the complexities of spatial intelligence and its pivotal role in shaping the future of technology.

Spatial intelligence, traditionally associated with the ability to visualize and manipulate objects and dimensions mentally, has found a new frontier in the realm of artificial intelligence. Here, it extends beyond human capabilities to empower machines and systems with the ability to perceive, understand, and interact with their environments in unprecedented ways. From self-driving cars navigating bustling city streets to robots performing complex surgeries, spatial intelligence facilitated by AI is setting the stage for a revolution in how machines operate and assist in our daily lives.

This book is designed not only to enlighten you with the theoretical underpinnings of spatial AI but also to engage you through direct insights into practical implementations. Whether you are a student aspiring to enter the field of AI, a professional looking to deepen your knowledge of contemporary AI applications, or simply a curious mind eager to understand how spatial reasoning is transforming our technological landscape, this book promises to be an invaluable resource.

Expect to encounter detailed discussions on:
- The fundamentals of spatial intelligence and its importance in AI.
- How AI systems utilize spatial data to make decisions and solve problems.
- Cutting-edge research and developments in robotics that exemplify the use of spatial intelligence.
- The impact of spatial AI on enhancing computer vision systems.
- The challenges and future potential of integrating AI with spatial intelligence in developing autonomous systems.

Throughout, "AI Spatial Intelligence Explained" maintains an approachable and engaging tone, making complex concepts accessible and demonstrating the tangible impacts of spatial AI through vivid examples. By the end, readers will not only have a comprehensive understanding of the subject but also an appreciation for how spatial intelligence is fundamentally transforming our approach to technology and innovation. Join us on this enlightening journey to explore how spatial intelligence, powered by artificial intelligence, is redefining the boundaries of what machines can achieve.

BASICS OF SPATIAL INTELLIGENCE

Spatial intelligence is a fundamental skill that profoundly influences both our daily lives and the technological landscape. This form of intelligence enables us to interpret and manage the spaces around us, from organizing a kitchen to navigating city streets. In technology, spatial intelligence is the backbone of innovations such as autonomous vehicles and augmented reality systems, where understanding the dimensions and dynamics of environmental interaction is crucial. By honing this ability, we sharpen our problem-solving skills and enhance our interaction with the physical world. This chapter dissects spatial intelligence into understandable components, elucidating how these elements shape our interaction with both familiar and complex environments. Through this understanding, we can appreciate the invisible yet significant role spatial intelligence plays in simplifying and structuring the chaos of our surroundings.

Imagine navigating through a bustling market where each stall is brimming with different goods, from fragrant spices to vibrant textiles. This scenario mirrors the essence of spatial intelligence—a cognitive skill that directs us in understanding and maneuvering effectively within spaces. Just as you would strategize your movements through the crowded aisles, anticipating where to turn or pause, spatial intelligence allows you to visualize and calculate your interactions with the environment around you. By envisioning the market as a grid or a map, you predict your path to avoid collisions and optimize your route to your desired location. This type of mental mapping isn't just limited to physical markets; it's similar to how we arrange furniture in a room to ensure enough walking space, or how a soccer player anticipates where to pass the ball on the field. Through such daily activities, we employ spatial intelligence not just to navigate but also to plan, solve spatial problems, and understand our surroundings in a more structured way. The concept might sound abstract, but in practice, it's as natural and necessary as plotting your course through that lively, chaotic market.

Spatial reasoning involves the mental processes used to manipulate information about objects' positions and dimensions, allowing individuals to navigate and organize their physical surroundings effectively. To illustrate, consider the act of parking a car in a tight space. This task requires one to estimate the car's size in relation to the parking spot, predict the trajectories as the car moves, and adjust accordingly to fit into the space without colliding with other vehicles or obstacles. Each decision in this process relies on spatial reasoning—estimating distances, visualizing the car's path, and adjusting strategies based on real-time feedback from the environment.

Similarly, planning a trip utilizes spatial visualization skills, where one must conceptualize various locations on a map and plot the most efficient routes. Here, you envision the layout of roads, landmarks, and destinations, even if you've never visited them, forming a mental map that guides your navigation decisions throughout the journey. This ability extends beyond physical travel to activities such as hiking or biking in unfamiliar terrain, where visualizing the environmental layout is critical for safety and efficiency.

In both scenarios, the fundamental processes involve visualizing, planning, and problem-solving within a spatial context. The ability to form mental images of different configurations and outcomes enables precise manipulation of these images to fit new conditions or requirements. This skill set demonstrates not just the capacity to handle immediate practical tasks, like fitting a car into a small parking space, but also the broader cognitive competence to navigate complex environments, which is indispensable in daily life and numerous professional fields. Through understanding and improving these capabilities, one gains not only a practical toolset for specific tasks but a robust framework for thinking and problem-solving that is widely applicable.

Let's take a deeper look at the cognitive processes involved in spatial reasoning, particularly when estimating dimensions and distances for tasks like parking a car or plotting a route. Initially, spatial reasoning relies heavily on the sensory input, primarily visual, that our brains receive from our surroundings. For instance, when you prepare to park in a tight spot, your eyes measure the relative sizes and distances of nearby cars, the parking space, and any obstacles. This visual information is quickly processed by the brain's occipital and parietal lobes, areas known for their roles in visual perception and spatial awareness.

Once this data is gathered, the brain shifts from simple perception to a more complex phase known as spatial visualization. Here, you use the visual data to construct a mental representation of your environment. In the context of driving, this means visualizing not only the current positions of surrounding objects but also predicting where they will move as you begin parking. This step is crucial because it allows you to simulate different outcomes based on potential movements you might make with the steering wheel.

Next, we move onto spatial orientation – deciding which way one needs to move or turn based on the mental model created. This phase involves interaction between the cognitive map in your brain and your decision-making processes, situated in the frontal cortex. Here, the brain calculates the best possible moves and visualizes the car's trajectory as you maneuver into the parking slot. It's an ongoing process of adjusting the mental map as you receive continuous feedback from your environment.

Finally, spatial reasoning culminates in the execution phase, where your decisions are translated into physical actions. For parking a car, this means turning the steering wheel, accelerating, or braking at just the right moments. The basal ganglia and cerebellum, parts of the brain responsible for movement control and coordination, play key roles here. They ensure that the actions you take align with the cognitive strategies and decisions formulated earlier.

Understanding this flow from sensory perception to physical action shows just how complex and dynamic our spatial reasoning abilities are. Even in ordinary activities like parking or navigating a new hiking trail, our brains are performing sophisticated calculations and adjustments. Grasping these processes gives us not only more appreciation for our cognitive capabilities but also insights into how we can train and improve these skills for better spatial awareness and decision-making in our daily lives.

Autonomous vehicles harness the power of spatial intelligence to navigate and make decisions in real time, a process crucial for safe and efficient transportation. At the core of this process is a suite of sensors and cameras that continuously collect data about the vehicle's surroundings. This data includes depth information, object recognition, and relative motion details, which are crucial for constructing an accurate three-dimensional map of the environment.

Once data collection is complete, the next stage involves translating this raw sensory input into actionable insights, a task managed by sophisticated onboard computers. These computers employ algorithms designed for pattern recognition and spatial awareness, processing the collected data to identify road boundaries, detect other vehicles, read traffic signs, and predict the actions of pedestrians and other obstacles.

The vehicle then uses these processed insights to make decisions. This involves a complex network of decision-making protocols that take into account current speeds, obstacle proximity, traffic laws, and predictive modelling of other road users' actions. For instance, if an autonomous vehicle detects a pedestrian stepping onto the road, it must decide whether to slow down, stop, or swerve, while also considering the speed and trajectory of nearby vehicles to avoid collisions.

Each of these decisions requires real-time computations that are heavily reliant on the vehicle's spatial intelligence capabilities. These systems must not only understand the current spatial arrangement but also anticipate future changes and adjust the vehicle's trajectory accordingly. The integration of these processes results in a seamless flow of operations that mimic a human driver's ability to navigate complex environments.

What makes autonomous driving particularly challenging—and fascinating—is the need for these systems to perform reliably under various and unpredictable environmental conditions. This ongoing interaction between sensor data and decision-making systems demonstrates the sophisticated application of spatial intelligence where every millisecond counts, and every decision can affect the safety and comfort of human passengers.

Understanding the intricacies of how these vehicles process and utilize spatial data not only highlights the advancements in artificial intelligence and robotics but also provides insights into how future technologies might continue to evolve and integrate into everyday human activities. This knowledge encourages a deeper appreciation of the technology's capabilities and its continuing improvement to meet real-world demands.

Autonomous vehicles rely heavily on advanced algorithms

and computational models to navigate through environments and make decisions in real time. The foundational elements of these systems include algorithms designed for object recognition and environmental mapping. These algorithms parse through raw sensor data collected from cameras, Lidar, radar, and other sensory devices to create a detailed map of the vehicle's surroundings. They categorize objects as either static, like road signs and traffic lights, or dynamic, such as pedestrians and other vehicles.

Object recognition algorithms typically use techniques from computer vision, often powered by deep learning frameworks, to identify and classify objects within the vehicle's field of view. Convolutional neural networks (CNNs), for example, are adept at processing pixel data from images to detect shapes and patterns that correspond to known objects. Meanwhile, environmental mapping might employ simultaneous localization and mapping (SLAM) techniques, which help in building a map of an unknown environment while also keeping track of the vehicle's location within that environment.

Decision-making models in autonomous vehicles then take this processed information to perform critical functions. These models consider several factors: compliance with traffic laws, obstacle avoidance capabilities, and predictive behaviors regarding other road users. For instance, if an algorithm detects a pedestrian stepping onto the road, the decision-making model evaluates possible actions—stopping, slowing down, or swerving—based on the current speed of the vehicle, the distance to the pedestrian, and the positions of nearby vehicles.

Machine learning plays a crucial role in refining these processes. Over time, machine learning algorithms analyze vast amounts of data collected during countless driving hours to improve the vehicle's decision-making accuracy. For example, by studying past instances where emergency braking was initiated, the system can better predict when to implement such measures in future situations. This ongoing learning process is vital for adapting to new or rare driving conditions that were not previously encountered.

The integration of these computational models—object recognition, environmental mapping, and decision-making—forms a cohesive system that allows autonomous vehicles to navigate safely and efficiently. By constantly collecting and analyzing data, and by learning from past experiences, these vehicles improve their ability to make intelligent decisions that ensure the safety of passengers and pedestrians alike. This cohesive operation showcases the remarkable capabilities of modern artificial intelligence implemented in real-world scenarios.

Enhancing spatial reasoning and visualization skills can be significantly beneficial, whether one is engaging in daily tasks or complex projects. A practical method to develop these capabilities involves participating in strategic video games or sports, which provide dynamic environments that require constant spatial decision-making and strategy formulation.

For instance, playing video games like 'Tetris' or 'Minecraft' compels the player to manipulate objects and navigate spaces in ways that exercise the brain's spatial reasoning faculties. In 'Tetris', one must fit falling shapes into a line at the bottom of the screen, a task that requires quick, precise judgments about spatial configurations. 'Minecraft', on the other hand, allows players to construct worlds using blocks, which necessitates envisioning and realizing spatial designs in a three-dimensional virtual environment.

Similarly, engaging in sports such as soccer or basketball also sharpens spatial skills. These sports demand an understanding of the playing field, the ability to anticipate the movements of other players, and the precise coordination of one's own movements. For example, a basketball player must gauge distances accurately to make successful passes and shots, while also visualizing the positions of teammates and opponents to execute effective game strategies.

Through these activities, individuals repeatedly simulate and solve spatial problems, which enhances their ability to visualize and manipulate both geometric figures and larger environments in real life. These exercises are not just forms of entertainment or physical engagement but are also substantial mental workouts that enhance cognitive functions critical in numerous professional and personal contexts. By incorporating such interactive and engaging tasks into regular routines, one not only bolsters spatial intelligence but also sets a foundation for better problem-solving and creative thinking in various aspects of daily life.

Imagine you're arranging furniture in your living room; deciding where each piece should go involves a kind of spatial intelligence very similar to more complex scenarios, like navigating a crowded subway system. Just as you must consider the size and function of a sofa or a coffee table to ensure everything fits comfortably and aesthetically in your room, navigating through a subway during rush hour requires quick thinking about your own space in relation to others, planning your route through the crowd to reach your train on time.

In both cases, you're predicting and visualizing spatial relationships, a fundamental aspect of spatial intelligence. Arranging a living room optimally requires envisioning different layouts and possibly rearranging items multiple times to find the most functional and pleasing configuration. This is akin to adjusting your path through the subway, anticipating the flow of the crowd, and adapting your movements based on real-time dynamics.

These everyday activities underscore the vital role of spatial intelligence not just in abstract or theoretical challenges but in practical, everyday decision-making. Whether it's organizing your living space or charting a path through a sea of people, the underlying cognitive processes are remarkably similar. They involve assessing the environment, visualizing potential scenarios, and making decisions that best utilize the available space. Through these analogies, the concept of spatial intelligence becomes not just understandable but intimately relatable, illuminating its presence and significance in everyday life.

Here is the detailed breakdown of the cognitive processes involved in spatial reasoning during everyday activities like arranging furniture or navigating crowded spaces:

- **<u>Perception</u>**: This initial stage involves the collection and recognition of sensory information relevant to spatial reasoning.
- **<u>Visual processing</u>**: The occipital lobe of the brain plays a crucial role here, interpreting visual stimuli to understand space and object positioning. It helps an individual assess dimensions and relative positions of objects in their field of view.
- **<u>Auditory cues</u>**: Sounds provide additional context in spatial assessments, especially in environments where visibility might be limited or obstructed. For example, in crowded places, auditory signals help gauge the density and movement of nearby people.

- **<u>Cognitive mapping</u>**: The brain's ability to create and update mental representations of surrounding environments.
- **<u>Memory integration</u>**: Both short-term and long-term memory are engaged in managing spatial information. Short-term memory allows for immediate recall of recent changes in the environment, while long-term memory holds more stable and extensive knowledge of familiar spaces.
- **<u>Adaptability</u>**: Cognitive maps are dynamic, updated continuously as new spatial data is perceived. This flexibility allows individuals to modify their internal maps promptly when navigating new spaces or when usual environments change.

- **<u>Decision-making</u>**: The process of evaluating potential actions based on current spatial understanding.

- **<u>Scenario simulation</u>**: The brain simulates various potential movements and outcomes using the current spatial data. This simulation helps in anticipating possible scenarios and planning movements or rearrangements effectively.

- **<u>Choice execution</u>**: Once a decision is made, it is translated into physical actions. This involves coordination with motor functions to navigate or arrange objects according to the chosen plan.

By examining these components in everyday scenarios, one gains a clearer and deeper understanding of how spatial intelligence operates seamlessly in our daily lives. This exploration enhances not just our knowledge but also appreciation of the sophisticated cognitive machinery at work when we perform simple tasks like arranging furniture or moving through a busy subway station. Understanding these processes in such detail ensures that the concept of spatial reasoning is not only comprehensible but also tangibly relatable, making its significance and application evident in various aspects of everyday living.

Spatial intelligence is a crucial cognitive skill that enables us to navigate and interact effectively with our surroundings. This ability impacts everything from performing simple tasks such as arranging furniture in a room to more complex challenges like navigating through a bustling city environment. By understanding and enhancing our spatial intelligence, we can improve our efficiency in daily activities and solve spatial problems more effectively.

At the core of spatial intelligence are the abilities to

perceive, reason, and visualize spatial relationships. These skills allow us to organize and manipulate our physical and mental perceptions of space. For instance, when planning a route in a crowded area, our mind has to account for various obstacles and adjust our path accordingly, showcasing our spatial reasoning in action.

Everyday activities offer numerous opportunities to practice and enhance these skills. Engaging in puzzles, playing spatially challenging games like chess, or participating in sports can all contribute to stronger spatial awareness. By actively fostering these abilities, we not only become better at navigating physical spaces but also sharpen our problem-solving and planning skills.

Incorporating an awareness of spatial intelligence into your everyday life not only simplifies daily tasks but also deepens your understanding of how we interact with the world around us. This knowledge isn't just theoretical; it has practical applications that can lead to more organized living spaces, smoother navigation, and more effective problem-solving strategies. So next time you're arranging your living space or planning a route through a crowded area, remember the power of spatial intelligence at your disposal.

SPATIAL AI IN ROBOTICS

Spatial intelligence, a pivotal force in the realm of robotics, enables machines to perceive, navigate, and interact with complex environments with precision and fineship. This chapter unravels the intricate dance of spatial AI in robotics, exploring how this sophisticated intelligence is not just about robots avoiding obstacles or charting paths but about transforming them into entities that can understand and adapt to the dynamics of real-world spaces. From industrial automation to autonomous vehicles, spatial AI facilitates a leap from programmed machines to intuitive, decision-making entities capable of understanding the depth, context, and nuances of their environments. Through a clear exploration of how these technologies are integrated and function within robotic systems, this discussion aims to shed light on the extraordinary capabilities of spatial AI, illustrating its profound impact on advancing robotic functionalities and its potential to revolutionize how machines operate and serve across various sectors.

Imagine you're trying to walk through a bustling market, navigating through stalls and people, deciding when to pause, speed up, or change direction based on the flow around you. This everyday task illustrates how robots use spatial intelligence to move and interact in their environments. Much like a person in a crowded market who uses sight, sound, and spatial awareness to avoid collisions and reach a desired location, robots are equipped with sensors and algorithms that help them perceive and understand their surroundings.

Robots use technologies such as LIDAR and computer vision to scan their environment continuously. These systems create a dynamic map of their surroundings, similar to how our brains construct a mental map of a new place. With these maps, robots can identify obstacles, measure distances, and plot courses with remarkable precision. The decisions made from this data are akin to a shopper weaving through a crowded aisle, adjusting their path in response to the movements of others around them.

This capability is crucial not just for navigating space but also for performing tasks that require interaction with objects and humans in that space. The practical application of this kind of spatial intelligence is immense—from autonomous cars navigating busy streets to robotic arms meticulously assembling intricate machinery. Thus, by understanding how robots use spatial intelligence akin to navigating a crowded market, we grasp a fundamental aspect of modern robotics, seeing its potential to enhance efficiencies and solve complex spatial challenges in numerous industries.

Here is the breakdown of sensor technologies and algorithms that empower robots with spatial intelligence, essential for navigation and interaction within their environments:

- **Sensor Technologies**: These are crucial for gathering spatial data, enabling robots to detect and navigate their surroundings effectively.

- **LIDAR**: Light Detection and Ranging (LIDAR) sensors emit laser beams to survey the environment. These lasers bounce off surfaces and return to the sensor, allowing the system to calculate distances by measuring the time each laser beam takes to return. This data is used to construct a detailed 3D map of the environment, which is crucial for navigation and obstacle avoidance.

- **Computer Vision**: Cameras serve as the eyes of a robot, capturing visual information from the environment. This visual data is then processed using image processing algorithms, which help in recognizing objects, mapping environments, and understanding the scene dynamics. These algorithms analyze pixel patterns to identify shapes, colors, and textures, contributing to the robot's comprehension of its surroundings.

- **Data Processing Algorithms**: Once data is collected by the sensors, these algorithms analyze and translate the raw data into actionable insights.

- **Data Integration**: This process involves merging information from multiple sensor types to form a unified and more accurate representation of the environment. For instance, data from LIDAR can be integrated with visual data from cameras to enhance the depth perception and detail in the environmental model that robots use to navigate.

- **Path Planning Algorithms**: These algorithms take the integrated sensor data and compute the safest and most efficient path for the robot to take. They consider variables such as distance, obstacles (both static like walls, and dynamic like moving people), and the robot's own physical capabilities. Algorithms such as A* (A-star), Dijkstra's, or

Rapidly-exploring Random Trees (RRT) are commonly used for this purpose. These computational methods evaluate multiple potential routes and choose the one that minimizes risks and maximizes efficiency based on the current environmental data.

This detailed explanation of the components involved in robotic spatial intelligence clarifies how these technologies and algorithms collectively enable robots to interpret and interact with their environment in a human-like manner, albeit relying on a complex backbone of sensors and computational theories. Understanding these mechanisms not only showcases the sophistication of modern robotics but also highlights the potential applications and enhancements these systems might bring to industries and daily life.

LIDAR technology, an acronym for Light Detection and Ranging, plays a pivotal role in the field of robotic navigation by providing precise, real-time environmental data that is crucial for autonomous decision-making. The operational essence of LIDAR involves emitting pulsed laser beams towards the surrounding areas. These pulses bounce back after hitting objects, and the LIDAR sensor calculates the time taken for each pulse to return. This time measurement is then used to determine the distance from the robot to various objects in its vicinity, effectively creating a detailed three-dimensional map of the environment.

The significance of LIDAR in robotics cannot be overstated, particularly in contexts where precision and safety are paramount. For instance, autonomous vehicles rely on LIDAR not only to navigate through complex urban and highway terrains but also to ensure safe interactions with pedestrians and other vehicles. By generating high-resolution maps of their surroundings, robots can identify and navigate around obstacles, anticipate changes in the environment, and make informed decisions about their path forward.

The process of converting raw LIDAR data into actionable navigation plans involves several sophisticated data processing steps. Each laser pulse's return time is compiled into a point cloud, a large dataset that represents the dispersed points in the three-dimensional space surrounding the robot. Advanced algorithms then interpret this point cloud to differentiate between static objects like buildings and dynamic entities such as moving vehicles, enhancing both the safety and efficiency of the robot's navigation strategies.

Moreover, the integration of LIDAR with other sensor technologies, like radar and cameras, enriches the robot's perceptual capabilities, allowing for more nuanced decision-making. For example, while LIDAR provides detailed distance data, cameras can offer complementary visual information that helps in object recognition, ensuring that the robot's understanding of its environment is both comprehensive and precise.

In conclusion, LIDAR's ability to provide accurate spatial data is indispensable for robots required to operate autonomously in complex, uncontrolled settings. Its role extends beyond mere data collection to fundamentally shaping the decision-making frameworks that govern autonomous robotic navigation, underscoring its critical importance in the advancement of robotic technologies.

When LIDAR sensors generate a point cloud, the data captured is extensive but raw, necessitating sophisticated algorithms to process and transform this information into a format useful for robotic navigation. Here's a detailed breakdown of how these algorithms work in sequence to enhance robotic capabilities:

Algorithms for Point Cloud Processing:
- **RANSAC (Random Sample Consensus):** This algorithm is used to identify and model the main structures within the point cloud by iteratively selecting a subset of data points and estimating parameters of a mathematical model (such as lines or planes). It is particularly effective in distinguishing between inlier points (points that fit the model) and outliers, which do not match the model and may represent noise or atypical points.
- **ICP (Iterative Closest Point):** ICP is essential for aligning multiple point clouds, a common requirement when LIDAR data is collected over time as a robot moves through its environment. The algorithm minimizes the difference between the corresponding points (usually the nearest neighbors) in the datasets, ensuring that the combined point cloud represents a cohesive and accurate model of the space.

Data Filtering and Noise Reduction:
- To improve the quality of the point cloud, raw data undergo stringent filtering processes. **Statistical Outlier**

Removal is one such technique that analyzes the variation in distances between neighboring points, removing points that deviate significantly from the average, thus cleaning the data of anomalies that could disrupt analysis.

Feature Extraction:
- The processed point cloud then undergoes feature extraction, where key navigational and environmental features such as edges, corners, and planes are identified. These features are crucial as they represent the boundaries and contours of objects and spaces, enabling robots to recognize and avoid obstacles and effectively map their surroundings.

Decision-Making Algorithms:
- The refined data is fed into decision-making algorithms which guide the robot's actions based on the interpreted surroundings.
- **Path Planning:** Algorithms like **Dijkstra's** or **A*** are employed to calculate the most efficient route from point A to point B within the mapped environment. They evaluate multiple paths based on the cost (which could represent distance, time, or energy required) and select the optimal route that avoids identified obstacles.
- **Obstacle Avoidance:** The **Dynamic Window Approach** is a technique used in real-time to adjust the robot's path in response to moving or sudden obstacles. It rapidly recalculates paths by predicting obstacle movements and assessing potential collision paths within a 'dynamic window' of safe trajectories.

This detailed layering of processes, from data capture to decision implementation, showcases the complexity and sophistication of how LIDAR and associated algorithms empower robots to navigate and interact autonomously in intricate environments. Understanding these steps offers insight into not only the mechanics of spatial data processing but also the strategic computations that support autonomous robot navigation, reflecting significant advancements in robotic AI technologies.

Spatial intelligence significantly enhances robotic capabilities in precise manipulation across diverse settings, such as manufacturing lines and healthcare facilities, where meticulous accuracy is mandatory. In manufacturing, robots equipped with advanced spatial intelligence systems use this intricate cognitive ability to interact with complex machinery and delicate components. For instance, in automotive assembly, robotic arms must position parts within millimetric precision, which necessitates robust spatial awareness and high-resolution tactile feedback. This feedback allows robots to adjust their grip and force, ensuring that components are assembled without damage.

In the realm of healthcare, spatial intelligence takes on a critical role in surgical robots. These robots leverage spatial data to navigate tight spaces and manipulate surgical tools with precision that surpasses human capability. Using 3D imaging and sensors that provide real-time feedback, surgical robots can perform intricate procedures, such as suturing tiny blood vessels or removing tumors in hard-to-reach areas, with minimal invasion and high accuracy.

The foundation of these advanced capabilities lies in the integration of tactile sensors and spatial data processing algorithms. These sensors not only detect the contact forces between the robot and its environment but also help in mapping the textures and shapes of the objects being manipulated. Algorithms interpret this sensor data to enable the robot to understand its spatial relation to the environment and any objects within it.

Furthermore, these systems continuously recalibrate and adjust their operations based on dynamic feedback. This adaptability is crucial in environments like operating theaters or high-precision manufacturing plants, where even minor deviations could have significant repercussions.

Understanding how spatial intelligence facilitates these operations underlines the importance of precise robotic manipulation. It not only enhances efficiency and safety in industries like manufacturing and healthcare but also pushes the boundaries of what is technologically possible, broadening the horizon for future innovations in robotic applications. This detailed exploration into the mechanics of spatial intelligence in robotic manipulation shows not just how it works but why it matters, providing insights that are crucial for both current applications and future advancements.

Let's take a closer look at the intricate technologies behind tactile sensors and spatial data processing algorithms in robotic systems, particularly in the realms of manufacturing and healthcare. These technologies not only enhance precision but are crucial to the functionality of robots performing complex tasks.

Tactile Sensors:

Tactile sensors in robotics are akin to the sense of touch in humans, enabling robots to detect and measure direct interaction with objects. Here's how they contribute:

- ### Types of Tactile Sensors:
  - **Capacitive Tactile Sensors:** These sensors detect changes in electrical capacitance caused by touch, often used to measure the deformation of the sensor surface when in contact with an object. This type is prevalent in applications requiring high sensitivity, such as in robotic fingers used in assembly lines.
  - **Resistive Tactile Sensors:** Constructed from conductive foam and electrodes, these sensors measure resistance changes when compressed. Common in industrial robotics, they are robust and suitable for environments where heavy interaction with objects is necessary.
  - **Optical Tactile Sensors:** Utilize changes in light transmission within the optical fibers under mechanical deformation to detect touch, offering advantages in precision and minimizing interference from external electronic noises. These are especially beneficial in medical robots during minimally invasive surgeries.

- ### Data Collection:
  - Tactile sensors measure nuances, such as different pressure levels and surface textures, providing vital data that robots use to adjust their grip on an object, prevent slippage, or identify the ideal amount of force needed for object

manipulation without causing damage.

Spatial Data Processing Algorithms:
- Data Integration:
- The spatial intelligence of a robot is largely derived from combining tactile feedback with other sensory data. For instance, integrating tactile data with visual input helps robots in healthcare precisely locate and suture soft tissues, combining feel and sight to achieve high accuracy.

- Real-time Adaptations:
- The core functionality of spatial data processing algorithms lies in their capacity to adapt in real-time. For example, fuzzy logic algorithms assess the degrees of truth rather than the fixed binary (true or false), allowing robots to make decisions in high-uncertainty environments effectively. They interpret various sensor inputs to enhance decision-making processes, adjusting robotic movements dynamically as per situational requirements.

Case Examples:
- In automotive manufacturing, tactile sensors equipped on robotic arms can precisely detect and adjust the pressure needed when installing sensitive components, like car windshields, ensuring proper installation without breakages.
- In healthcare, surgical robots equipped with optical tactile sensors perform delicate procedures within cramped spaces of the human body, providing surgeons a high-resolution tactile image of the operation site, crucial for tasks requiring utmost delicacy and precision.

These examples and detailed insights into tactile sensors and processing algorithms reveal the sophistication and critical roles these technologies play in robotic operations. They allow robots not just to perform tasks but to excel with an accuracy and sensitivity akin to or surpassing human capabilities. This understanding helps appreciate the nuanced complexities of modern robotics and the profound impact these technologies have on industries where precision is paramount.

The integration of visual, auditory, and tactile data in robotic systems exemplifies a sophisticated level of sensory fusion, crucial for enabling adaptive and responsive behaviors in dynamic environments. Each type of sensor data plays a distinct role, collectively providing a comprehensive perception system that mimics human sensory capabilities.

Visual sensors in robots typically involve cameras and sometimes LIDAR systems that provide detailed images and spatial data of the environment. This visual information helps in identifying obstacles and navigating through spaces. For example, visual data allows a robotic vacuum to detect furniture and avoid collisions while cleaning a room.

Auditory sensors, on the other hand, detect sound waves, which can be crucial for operations in environments where sound provides essential cues. Consider a factory robot that can listen for machine malfunctions signaled by unusual sounds, enabling early detection and response before a breakdown occurs.

Tactile sensors deal with physical interaction with the environment. Robots equipped with tactile sensors can feel the texture, shape, and hardness of objects they interact with, similar to how a person might use their sense of touch to verify the ripeness of a fruit. For instance, a robot in an assembly line uses tactile feedback to determine the correct force needed to place a delicate component without causing damage.

The process of integrating these sensory inputs involves data fusion algorithms that enable the robot to build a unified and real-time understanding of its surroundings. These algorithms process the data streams continuously, merging them into a cohesive model that guides the robot's decisions and actions. For example, in a rescue operation, a robot might visually identify obstacles, listen for sounds of people calling for help, and feel its way through debris, effectively combining all sensory data to navigate and perform its tasks.

This integration allows robotic systems to adapt their behavior based on comprehensive situational awareness. As environments change, the systems can recalibrate their responses, using updated data to optimize navigation strategies, interaction methods, and operational tasks. The adaptive nature of this sensory integration is crucial in environments that are unstructured and unpredictable, where rigid programming alone would fail to achieve efficient outcomes.

Understanding how these various forms of data come together in robotic systems not only highlights the advanced level of current technology but also opens up possibilities for future innovations that could further enhance the versatility and effectiveness of robots in an array of complex environments. This sophisticated sensory integration underscores the ongoing advancements in robotics, pushing the boundaries of how machines perceive and interact with the world.

Let's explore the sophisticated data fusion algorithms utilized in robotic systems for integrating visual, auditory, and tactile data, enhancing robots' ability to understand and interact with their environments effectively.

Specific Algorithms:

These data fusion algorithms are pivotal in creating a more coherent understanding of a robot's environment by integrating diverse sensory inputs:

- **Kalman Filters**: These are used extensively in robotics for their efficiency in predicting future states of a moving object. Kalman Filters operate by forming estimates of an unknown variable by blending measured data over time, accounting for noise and other inaccuracies. This method is particularly useful in applications such as navigation, where the position and direction of a robot must be continuously updated.

- **Bayesian Networks**: These probabilistic models are vital for handling uncertainty in sensory data. Bayesian

Networks aid robots in making informed decisions by employing Bayesian inferences, which update the probability of a hypothesis as more evidence or information becomes available. This approach is beneficial when dealing with ambiguous data from sensors, helping the robot to decide based on the most probable scenario.

- **Neural Networks**: Especially deep learning models, are crucial for processing complex patterns within large datasets. In robotic systems, neural networks analyze inputs from various sensors to learn and make sense of intricate patterns, enhancing the robot's perception and response strategies. These networks are particularly adept at tasks involving image recognition, vital for interpreting visual data.

Integration Process:

The integration of data from various sensor systems into a unified model involves several critical processes:

- **Data Synchronization**: For effective data fusion, it is essential to align data from different sensors temporally. This synchronization ensures that the input data are integrated in a coherent and timely manner, providing accurate and contextually relevant environmental models to the robot.

- **Error Reduction**: Algorithms are employed to refine the sensor data, reducing noise and potential errors that could affect the robot's decision-making process. Techniques such as smoothing and outlier detection are commonly used to enhance the quality of the data inputs before they are used in further analysis.

Application Examples:

Data fusion algorithms enable robots to perform effectively in dynamic and unpredictable environments:

- **Rescue Robots**: In disaster scenarios, rescue robots combine spatial, auditory, and visual cues to navigate through debris, using integrated data to locate survivors. The fusion of tactile feedback with auditory and visual data allows these robots to maneuver safely and efficiently in collapsed structures.

- **Autonomous Vehicles**: For self-driving cars, the integration of sensory data is crucial for safe navigation in complex traffic conditions. These vehicles rely on combined inputs from cameras, radar, and ultrasonic sensors to perceive traffic patterns, detect obstacles, and adapt driving strategies in real-time.

This detailed examination of data fusion algorithms highlights how various interconnected processing layers work together to enhance robotic functionalities. By understanding these foundational technologies, one gains insight into how modern robotics achieve high levels of adaptability and precision, crucial for operating effectively across a spectrum of industrial and commercial applications.

Imagine you're navigating through a crowded city street in your car, making split-second decisions based on the flow of traffic, pedestrians crossing, and unexpected obstacles.

This daily driving challenge mirrors the complex world of autonomous vehicles powered by spatial AI. Just as you use your senses and judgment to weave through traffic smoothly, autonomous vehicles use a suite of sensors and algorithms to perceive and navigate their environment safely.

In the realm of autonomous vehicles, companies like Tesla and Waymo serve as compelling case studies. These vehicles integrate cameras, radar, and LIDAR to construct a detailed, real-time map of their surroundings. The spatial AI then processes this data to make informed decisions, such as accelerating, braking, or swerving to avoid collisions. For example, when faced with a sudden obstruction, similar to a driver spotting a fallen tree branch, the vehicle's spatial AI calculates the safest maneuver around the obstacle without compromising the comfort of passengers. This technology doesn't just mimic human reflexes—it optimizes them, enhancing safety and efficiency on a scale that humans alone couldn't achieve.

Switching gears to industrial settings, consider a robot in a manufacturing plant, much like a skilled worker specializing in assembling complex machinery parts. Here, robots equipped with spatial AI might work on intricate tasks such as assembling electronic components. These robots use tactile sensors and precise movement control to handle and assemble parts accurately, minimizing the risk of errors and waste. For instance, it's akin to a watchmaker assembling a clock, where meticulous attention to detail is paramount. Only, in this case, the robot can work tirelessly around the clock, boosting productivity and maintaining consistent quality.

These real-world applications of spatial AI in autonomous vehicles and industrial robots illustrate not just the technology's ability to solve complex problems but also its potential to transform industries. By improving precision and efficiency, spatial AI opens up new possibilities for innovation and optimization, making operations safer, faster, and more cost-effective. This evolution of technology shows us a glimpse of how the future of automation in motion and production will continue to evolve, making the mechanics behind everyday activities both fascinating and increasingly reliant on intelligent systems.

Let's take a deeper look at the intricate sensors and algorithms that empower autonomous vehicles and industrial robots with precision and intelligence for navigating and executing tasks efficiently.

Types of Sensors Used in Autonomous Vehicles:

- **Cameras**: Cameras are pivotal for providing visual data, acting as the eyes of the vehicle. They capture detailed images that help in recognizing objects, traffic signs, and lane markings, which are crucial for situational awareness and decision-making. This visual data is processed to identify stationary and moving obstacles, aiding in safe and efficient navigation through diverse environments.

- **Radar**: Radar technology plays a critical role by emitting radio waves that reflect off objects, measuring their distance and relative speed to the vehicle. This capability is vital for adaptive cruise control systems and emergency braking, as it helps in understanding the dynamic environment, especially in poor visibility conditions.

- **LIDAR**: LIDAR sensors contribute by emitting pulsed laser beams to create a 360-degree, three-dimensional map of the vehicle's surroundings. This high-resolution map is key for autonomous vehicles to make accurate navigation decisions, helping in the detection of road edges, pedestrian paths, and unforeseen obstructions.

Algorithms in Autonomous Driving:
- Object Detection Algorithms:
- **YOLO (You Only Look Once)** and **SSD (Single Shot MultiBox Detector)** are two widely used algorithms that process data from cameras for real-time object detection. YOLO is known for its speed and efficiency in detecting objects in a single sweep of the image, while SSD provides a good balance between speed and accuracy, crucial for dynamic driving scenarios.

- Path Planning Algorithms:
- **RRT (Rapidly Exploring Random Tree)** and **Dijkstra's Algorithm** are used to compute the safest and most efficient paths by exploring various routes and selecting the optimal path that avoids obstacles. These algorithms are fundamental in scenarios where quick recalculations are necessary due to sudden changes in the environment.

Use of Tactile Sensors in Industrial Robots:
- Tactile sensors enable robots to detect the physical properties of objects they interact with. They provide critical

data on the texture, hardness, and precise dimensions, enabling robots to adjust their grip and apply the correct amount of force, significantly reducing the risk of damaging delicate components during assembly tasks.

Data Integration and Real-time Response Algorithms:

- The integration of tactile, auditory, and visual data is managed through advanced fusion algorithms, which analyze and merge information to make real-time decisions. Techniques like **Bayesian Networks** and **Neural Networks** are utilized to predict outcomes based on this integrated data, enhancing the robot's decision-making capabilities.

Real-world Examples:

- In urban settings, a **Tesla Model X** uses an amalgamation of these sensory inputs and algorithms to thread through traffic, detect pedestrians, and even park itself autonomously.
- In industrial environments, robots like those from **Fanuc** utilize similar technologies to enhance efficiencies on production lines, where precision is key to assembling parts of automobiles or electronics without errors.

These examples and detailed insights into the array of sensors and algorithms illustrate how cutting-edge technologies are revolutionizing the fields of autonomous driving and robotic automation, paving the way for smarter, safer, and more efficient operations across many sectors.

Robotic spatial intelligence stands at a transformative juncture, with current trends indicating a robust integration of more advanced sensory technologies and AI-driven analytics into robotic systems. These innovations are set to enhance the capabilities of robots in interpreting and interacting with their environments in increasingly sophisticated ways.

One of the most significant trends is the development of deep learning techniques that allow robots to not only collect but also interpret vast amounts of spatial data with a high degree of accuracy. This ability leads to more nuanced decision-making and adaptive behaviors in dynamic environments. As robots become more proficient in handling unpredictability, their applications expand beyond traditional manufacturing and into domains such as domestic service, elderly care, and even complex medical procedures.

However, these advancements also bring forth challenges. For instance, the integration of complex systems increases the risk of cybersecurity threats. Malicious entities could exploit vulnerabilities, leading to potential safety hazards. Additionally, as robots become more autonomous, ethical concerns such as privacy invasion and unemployment due to automation become more prominent. Addressing these issues requires not only technological solutions but also robust legal frameworks and ethical guidelines to ensure that the development of robotic technologies aligns with societal values and norms.

Moreover, there is the challenge of data overload. As spatial intelligence systems collect more detailed and frequent data, managing this vast influx of information without overwhelming the processing capabilities of robots or infringing on privacy becomes critical.

In response to these challenges, future innovations may focus on developing more efficient data processing algorithms and safer, more resilient integration frameworks. Researchers are also exploring new forms of human-robot interaction to ensure that these advanced machines act in ways that are beneficial and acceptable to society.

Overall, the trajectory of robotic spatial intelligence promises exciting possibilities for progress in automation and artificial intelligence. However, navigating this path will require careful consideration of the potential consequences and proactive strategies to mitigate risks.

COMPUTER VISION AND SPATIAL AI

In the intricate dance of modern technology, computer vision and spatial AI play pivotal roles. These technologies empower machines to interpret and interact with our world in fundamentally sophisticated ways. Through the lens of computer vision, machines capture and analyze visual data, much like human beings utilize their eyes to perceive their surroundings. When this capability is enhanced with spatial AI, these systems not only see but also understand the dimensions and dynamics of the space around them. This combination creates a comprehensive sensory experience, allowing machines from autonomous vehicles to robotic assistants to navigate and operate within complex environments accurately.

This profound synergy between computer vision and spatial intelligence opens up unprecedented possibilities for automation and enhances interactions between humans and machines. It ensures tasks such as navigating through traffic, performing delicate surgeries, or managing warehouses are carried out with greater precision and efficiency. Each application speaks directly to the remarkable versatility and potential of spatial AI to revolutionize industries and daily life. By examining how these technologies are applied, we gain insights into the sophisticated architecture of machine perception and operation, highlighting the transformative impact of combining visual data with spatial awareness.

Spatial intelligence in AI systems fundamentally enhances

how machines perceive and interact with their environment, focusing on essential processes such as depth perception and object recognition. This intelligence allows machines to not only capture images but also to understand and navigate the space within these images. For instance, consider depth perception, a process similar to how a person can judge the distance of an object like a moving car or a staircase step. In AI, this is achieved through technologies like stereo vision, where two cameras capture the same scene from slightly different angles, mimicking human binocular vision. The AI analyzes the variations between these images to gauge depth, which is critical for tasks requiring precise spatial awareness, such as autonomous driving or robotic surgery.

Moving to object recognition, this process allows AI systems to identify and classify objects within their visual field. This capability can be likened to recognizing faces in a crowded room. Here, AI uses algorithms such as Convolutional Neural Networks (CNNs) that have been trained on thousands of images to detect patterns that differentiate one object from another. These algorithms analyze various aspects of an object, such as shape, size, and color, to accurately identify and categorize it in real-time, which is vital for applications such as automated quality control in manufacturing or sorting systems in logistics.

Together, depth perception and object recognition illustrate the profound capability of spatial intelligence to transform a simple visual input into a rich, three-dimensional understanding. This enhanced perception allows AI systems to make informed decisions based on the layout and objects within their environment, facilitating more interactive and autonomous operations. As this technology continues to evolve, it promises to refine further how machines understand and navigate our world, marking a significant leap toward more advanced and intuitive AI systems.

Let's take a detailed look at how stereo vision and convolutional neural networks (CNNs) fundamentally empower AI systems in understanding and interacting with their environments.

Stereo Vision:

Stereo vision systems mimic the human binocular vision, utilizing two cameras positioned at slightly different angles to capture the same scene. This setup allows AI to interpret depth in a manner similar to how humans perceive three-dimensional space.

- **Camera Calibration and Synchronization**: Before capturing images, stereo vision systems need to ensure that both cameras are perfectly calibrated and synchronized. Calibration involves adjusting each camera to ensure that they both point at the same object from different angles without any parallax error, which is critical for accurate depth measurement. Synchronization ensures that images are captured simultaneously to maintain consistency in the dynamic analysis.

- **Disparity Map Creation**: Once the images are captured, the system computes a disparity map by measuring the pixel difference (disparity) between corresponding points in the left and right images. The disparity is inversely proportional to the scene's depth at each pixel, allowing the AI to determine how far away each part of the scene is from the observer. This process can be likened to how our brain calculates depth by comparing the different images received from our left and right eyes.

- **Depth Decision Algorithms**: Algorithms then analyze the disparity map to make depth-related decisions. Techniques like Block Matching, which searches for corresponding blocks between two stereo images, and Semi-Global Matching, which considers pixel disparities in multiple directions for smoother and more accurate depth perception, are employed to interpret these maps.

Convolutional Neural Networks (CNNs) for Object Recognition:

CNNs are specialized deep learning algorithms used to recognize and classify objects within images through a series of convolutional, pooling, and fully connected layers.

- **Architecture Breakdown**:
- **Convolutional Layers**: These layers apply numerous filters to the input image, creating feature maps that capture key features such as edges, colors, or textures.
- **Pooling Layers**: Following convolution, pooling layers reduce the dimensionality of each feature map, condensing the information to the most essential elements, thus improving computational efficiency.
- **Fully Connected Layers**: These layers act as a classifier on top of the features extracted by the convolutional and pooling layers. They analyze the global

patterns to determine the object's class within the image.

   - **Training Process**: CNNs undergo training using vast datasets of labeled images, where each label corresponds to the object in the image. Through a process called backpropagation, CNNs learn by continuously adjusting the weights of the network to minimize the difference between the predicted output and the actual label.

   - **Role of Activation and Loss Functions**: Activation functions introduce non-linear properties to the network, helping it learn complex patterns. Loss functions, on the other hand, provide a mechanism to measure the accuracy of the output, guiding the network on how to improve during the training phase by minimizing error.

   Understanding these technological foundations highlights the sophistication of spatial intelligence in AI systems. This exploration not only clarifies the operations of these advanced systems but also underscores their transformative potential in industries ranging from automotive to healthcare, showcasing a future where AI's visual and spatial understanding significantly impacts our interaction with technology.

   Key technologies such as LIDAR, stereo cameras, and advanced algorithms play pivotal roles in enhancing the spatial awareness of AI systems. Each technology contributes uniquely to how machines perceive and navigate the three-dimensional space around them.

LIDAR, or Light Detection and Ranging, uses laser light to map out the environment. This technology emits thousands of laser beams every second and measures how long it takes for each beam to bounce back after hitting an object. This data is then used to create a precise three-dimensional map of the surroundings. For example, similar to how echolocation works for bats, LIDAR allows autonomous vehicles to "see" the road, identify obstacles like pedestrians and other vehicles, and navigate safely.

Stereo cameras, on the other hand, utilize two cameras, much like human eyes, positioned a short distance apart. They capture two slightly differing images simultaneously. Specialized software processes these images to find matching points between them and calculate the depth of each point, a method known as stereo vision. This process is similar to how viewing through binoculars offers a more profound sense of depth compared to using a monocular scope. This depth perception is crucial for tasks requiring detailed spatial understanding, such as robotic surgery or precision robotics in manufacturing.

Advanced algorithms, including those used in machine learning and computer vision, process and interpret the vast amounts of data generated by sensors like LIDAR and stereo cameras. These algorithms identify patterns, make predictions, and learn from new data, continuously improving their accuracy. For instance, consider how a GPS system learns the best routes over time; similarly, these algorithms optimize how AI systems respond to their environments, leading to more effective decision-making and autonomous operation.

Together, LIDAR, stereo cameras, and sophisticated algorithms ensure AI systems have a nuanced understanding of their physical surroundings. This capability is akin to giving machines a sense of touch, sight, and intuition all rolled into one, allowing them to interact with the world in ways previously limited to science fiction. As these technologies advance, they promise to further refine how AI systems function, making them increasingly integral to industries where automation and precision are paramount.

LIDAR, stereo cameras, and advanced algorithms form a cohesive integration within AI systems, enabling them to navigate and understand their environments with remarkable precision and efficiency. Here's a detailed breakdown of how these components operate and interact:

LIDAR Operation in AI Systems:
- **Data Acquisition:** LIDAR systems function by sending out multiple laser beams into the environment. These lasers reflect off surfaces and return to the sensor. The system measures the time it takes for each laser to return, which is directly correlated to the distance of the object from the sensor.
- **Data Processing:** The raw data collected by the LIDAR, primarily the time measurements, are converted into a three-dimensional model of the environment, known as a point cloud. This conversion involves calculating the distance based on the speed of light and the time delay, arranging these points in three-dimensional space to reflect their real-world positions.
- **Integration and Utilization:** The structured point cloud data is then fed into the AI system's central processing

unit. Here, it is used for critical functionalities such as detecting obstacles, assessing the layout of the environment, and planning navigational paths. This data is integral for the AI to make informed decisions about its movements and interactions within its surroundings.

Stereo Cameras in AI Systems:
- **Image Capture and Synchronization:** Stereo cameras, set up at a fixed distance apart, capture two images of the same scene from slightly different angles. Precise synchronization ensures that the images correspond temporally, providing a coherent view for depth analysis.
- **Depth Mapping:** These dual images are then analyzed using stereo matching algorithms, which find similar points between the two images and calculate the depth by examining the disparity in their positions. The greater the disparity, the closer the object is to the cameras.
- **Utilization in AI Systems:** The depth information gleaned from stereo cameras is merged with data from other sensors, including LIDAR. This fusion provides a robust spatial understanding, allowing for dynamic adjustments to the device's path and interactions in real-time, thereby enhancing operational safety and effectiveness.

Role of Advanced Algorithms in AI Systems:
- **Pattern Recognition:** Machine learning algorithms, particularly convolutional neural networks (CNNs), play a crucial role in processing visual data from cameras—both stereo and conventional. These networks can recognize and classify various objects by identifying unique patterns and features in the visual data they receive.
- **Predictive Analytics:** The system employs these

algorithms to analyze historical and real-time data to predict likely scenarios and make preemptive decisions. This capability is vital in dynamic environments where conditions change rapidly.

- **Integration of Multiple Data Sources:** Advanced algorithms synthesize the data from LIDAR, stereo cameras, and other sensors. This integrated data analysis helps the AI system to comprehensively understand its environment and make informed decisions based on a complete view of its surroundings.

In conclusion, the synergy between LIDAR, stereo cameras, and advanced algorithms equips AI systems with a sophisticated toolkit to interpret complex environments, making decisions that are not just reactive but also predictive and informed. These technologies, combined in an intelligent manner, lay a solid foundation for the autonomy of machines in navigating our world.

Imagine you're smoothly navigating through city traffic in a self-driving car, thanks to the unseen but vigilant eyes of spatial AI. This scenario isn't too different from a skilled driver who deftly maneuvers through rush hour, constantly adjusting speed and steering based on the surrounding cars, pedestrians, and changing signals. In autonomous driving, spatial AI serves a similar role but does so with a blend of advanced sensors and algorithms. It uses technologies like LIDAR and stereo cameras, functioning much like a combination of human eyesight and intuition, to scan the road. This continuous scan helps the AI to understand the car's environment in three dimensions and make immediate decisions, such as when to slow down for a jaywalker or how best to avoid an unexpected roadblock.

Now, think about a factory where robots sort packages. Imagine how effortlessly a person can pick different objects from a moving conveyor belt, recognizing items based on size, shape, and perhaps labeled destination, and then placing them into the correct bins. Spatial AI equips robots with a similar discernment ability, allowing them to identify and sort objects at high speeds with precision. This is achieved through cameras calibrated with machine learning models that instruct the robots on recognizing various objects and deciding where they need to be routed. It's analogous to having an extremely attentive and unfailing postal worker who never misses a detail.

In both cases, spatial AI is crucial for tasks that require an acute awareness of space and the ability to process visual information in real time. Whether it's guiding a car or sorting objects in a factory, spatial AI applies its "learned" knowledge to make real-world interactions smoother and more efficient. These examples highlight not just the functioning but also the profound impact of spatial intelligence in transforming mundane tasks into automated, precision-driven processes. This evolution in routine and critical operations underscores the seamless integration of AI into the fabric of daily technological interactions, presenting a blend of cutting-edge sophistication and practical utility.

Here is the detailed breakdown of how spatial AI technologies operate in autonomous vehicles and automated manufacturing systems:

- **Autonomous Vehicles:**
- **LIDAR:**
- **Functionality:** LIDAR systems function by emitting light pulses and measuring the time it takes for them to bounce back after hitting surrounding objects. This technology provides a real-time, high-resolution, three-dimensional map of the vehicle's surroundings, critical for understanding complex environments.
- **Data Processing:** The raw data collected from LIDAR, which includes distance measurements based on light travel time, is processed and transformed into a 3D spatial map. This map is crucial for the vehicle, aiding in navigation and identifying obstacles efficiently.

- **Stereo Cameras:**
- **Image Capture:** Stereo cameras, installed at strategic points on the vehicle, capture the same scene from slightly different angles. This setup mimics human binocular vision and is essential for depth perception.
- **Data Integration:** The captured images are synthesized using advanced image processing algorithms. This integration helps the system to assess depth and spatial relationships in real-time, enabling dynamic and safe decision-making on the road.

- **Machine Learning Models:**
- **Object Recognition:** Using intricate pattern recognition algorithms, such as convolutional neural networks, the AI system identifies and classifies various entities like road signs, pedestrians, and other vehicles. This capability is fundamental for active and safe navigation.
- **Predictive Modelling:** The AI incorporates historical data along with real-time sensory inputs to predict

potential road hazards and determine optimal routes, enhancing both safety and efficiency.

- **Automated Manufacturing Systems:**
  - **Spatial Recognition:**
    - **Camera Setups:** Several high-definition cameras are strategically deployed around the manufacturing area to capture detailed visuals of the production environment. This setup allows the system to monitor and analyze the operational area continuously.
    - **Object Differentiation:** AI algorithms process the visual data to distinguish between different items based on size, shape, and labeled characteristics. This differentiation is crucial for precise sorting and handling of materials.

  - **Machine Learning Integration:**
    - **Training Models:** AI systems are trained on vast datasets containing images and characteristics of manufacturing components. This training enables the AI to recognize and handle various components correctly.
    - **Decision Algorithms:** The system uses sophisticated decision-making algorithms to guide robotic actions for detailed tasks, such as sorting and assembling parts. These algorithms optimize the manufacturing process, ensuring efficiency and accuracy.

Each component, meticulously designed and integrated, enables sophisticated AI operations in handling real-world challenges encountered in autonomous driving and manufacturing scenarios. This meticulous orchestration of technologies not only showcases the advanced capabilities of spatial AI but also underscores its growing importance in the technological landscape.

Integrating artificial intelligence into our daily lives presents a set of significant challenges that range from technical hurdles to ethical concerns. A primary issue is data privacy. AI systems require vast amounts of data to learn and make decisions. When this data pertains to personal or sensitive information, it raises concerns about how it is collected, used, and stored. For instance, consider a smart home assistant that learns from daily interactions with its users. The convenience it offers must be balanced with the assurance that the users' information remains private and protected under stringent data security measures.

Another considerable challenge is the sheer computational power needed to operate sophisticated AI algorithms effectively. High-level AI processing demands substantial computing resources which can be costly and energy-intensive. This requirement can lead to increased carbon footprints, counteracting sustainability efforts. To illustrate, training a single AI model can consume as much electricity as several homes use in one year.

Furthermore, seamlessly integrating AI into human environments brings its own set of challenges. AI needs to operate in a way that complements human behaviors and societal norms. For example, consider autonomous vehicles in urban settings. These vehicles must not only navigate safely but also adapt to social driving behaviors, understanding human road signals and gestures which are often not standardized.

Addressing these challenges requires careful consideration of the design, implementation, and governance of AI technologies. Solutions might include developing more energy-efficient processing methods, enacting policies that protect personal data, and designing AI systems that enhance rather than disrupt social structures. By tackling these issues head-on, we can ensure that AI technologies are developed and deployed in ways that are ethical, sustainable, and beneficial to society, making advanced AI a responsible and valuable tool in modern technology landscapes.

Let's take a closer look at the advanced measures and technologies AI systems use to manage data privacy, enhance computational efficiency, and seamlessly adapt to human environments.

Data Privacy in AI Systems:
- Encryption Techniques:
- Advanced Encryption Standard (AES) and Rivest-Shamir-Adleman (RSA) are two primary encryption algorithms widely used to secure data. AES is known for its speed and efficiency in handling large volumes of data, making it a popular choice for securing online data at rest. Conversely, RSA is used primarily for secure data transmissions, thanks to its robust public-key encryption which ensures that only the intended recipient can decrypt the message.
- Data Anonymization Processes:
- Prior to analysis, sensitive data undergoes anonymization to strip any personally identifiable information. Techniques such as adding noise to data,

generalization where details are replaced with less precise but still accurate data, or pseudonymization where personal identifiers are replaced with artificial identifiers, are commonly employed. This ensures that the data remains useful for analysis without compromising individual privacy.

- **Regulatory Compliance:**

- AI systems are meticulously designed to comply with stringent international data protection regulations. Compliance with the General Data Protection Regulation (GDPR) in the EU, or the Health Insurance Portability and Accountability Act (HIPAA) in the US, involves implementing measures such as data minimization, securing consent before data processing, and maintaining transparent data processing and storage procedures.

Computational Efficiency in AI:
- **Emerging Technologies:**

- Field-Programmable Gate Arrays (FPGAs) and Application-Specific Integrated Circuits (ASICs) are at the forefront in reducing the power consumption for AI processes. Unlike general-purpose processors, FPGAs and ASICs are customized to perform specific functions more efficiently—speeding up data processing while using less power.

- **Algorithm Optimization:**

- Techniques such as model pruning, which removes unnecessary or redundant data from training models without losing their predictive accuracy, and quantization, which reduces the precision of the model's parameters, significantly cut down the computational load. These methods ensure that AI models remain both high-performing and resource-efficient.

AI Adaptation to Human Environments:
- Behavioral Modeling:
- AI systems delve into behavioral modeling by analyzing vast amounts of data on human interactions and behavioral patterns. By employing machine learning algorithms, these systems can predict and mimic human behaviors, making AI-driven applications like virtual assistants more intuitive and personalized.
- Interactive Learning:
- Through techniques such as reinforcement learning and human-in-the-loop feedback systems, AI continuously learns and adapts to its operational environment. This interactive learning enables AI systems to refine their algorithms based on real-time human interactions, improving their decision-making processes and making their services more aligned with human needs and preferences.

These intricate components and processes showcase the depth of technology's integration into AI systems, ensuring they operate effectively within our societal frameworks and personal lives. By understanding these mechanisms, we can appreciate the sophistication of current AI technologies and their impact on daily interactions and systemic operations.

Emerging technological trends are reshaping the landscape of artificial intelligence and automation, heralding a future where machine autonomy and interactive environments reach unprecedented levels. These advancements, rooted in the accelerating capabilities of AI and robotics, promise to deliver more intuitive, autonomous machines that can seamlessly interact with human environments and cater to our needs with minimal input.

In the near future, machine autonomy will advance beyond simple task execution to complex decision-making situations. Current developments in AI, particularly in deep learning and neural networks, are paving the way for machines that can independently analyze situations, learn from new experiences, and make decisions that once required human judgment. For example, autonomous vehicles will not only navigate traffic but will make real-time decisions about route changes based on weather conditions, traffic updates, and passenger preferences.

Simultaneously, the rise of enhanced interactive artificial environments is set to revolutionize the way we live and work. These environments will use sophisticated sensory inputs and AI to create spaces that respond dynamically to human presence and interaction. Imagine walking into a room that adjusts lighting, temperature, and even background music based on your mood, detected through biometric signals, or a virtual meeting space that can replicate the physical presence of participants from around the globe.

These technological strides are not just enhancements but transformative shifts that promise to redefine boundaries between humans and machines, making our interactions with devices more natural and intuitive. As these technologies continue to evolve and integrate, they will undoubtedly open new avenues for innovation, fundamentally altering our daily lives and workspaces.

The integration of spatial intelligence with computer vision marks a significant leap in how machines interpret and interact with their environment. This fusion creates systems capable of understanding and navigating three-dimensional spaces with a level of precision and autonomy that mirrors human perception. The application of these technologies transforms various sectors, enhancing the functionality of autonomous vehicles, improving the efficiency of automated manufacturing processes, and even redefining interactive environments for enhanced human-computer interaction.

Spatial intelligence enables devices to measure and interpret every component of their surroundings, from the layout of a room to the movements of nearby objects and people. When combined with the analytical power of computer vision, these systems not only see but also comprehend and predict, allowing them to make smarter decisions in real time. For example, in autonomous driving, this integration allows vehicles to understand road conditions, detect obstacles, and navigate safely by continuously adapting to new sensory information.

This chapter has explored both the technical underpinnings and practical applications of this transformative integration, illustrating its vast potential. As these technologies continue to evolve, they promise to further dissolve the boundaries between digital computation and real-world application, making intelligent systems more effective collaborators in our daily lives. This not only streamlines tasks and operations across multiple industries but also ushers in new realms of innovation where human and machine capabilities complement each other, leading to unprecedented levels of efficiency and innovation.

AUTONOMOUS VEHICLES AND SPATIAL REASONING

Spatial reasoning stands as a cornerstone technology that powers the brains of autonomous vehicles, enabling them to interpret and navigate through complex environments efficiently. This technology equips vehicles with the ability to make sense of their surroundings, process vast amounts of spatial data, and make split-second decisions that ensure safe and smooth navigation. At its core, spatial reasoning allows these vehicles to 'see' and 'understand' the road in a way that is remarkably similar to human perception, but with the added reliability and precision offered by advanced computing.

Spatial reasoning in autonomous vehicles hinges on the integration of sensors, cameras, and intricate algorithms to continuously assess and respond to dynamic conditions. Whether it's dodging an unforeseen obstacle on the highway or choosing the best path through an urban maze, spatial reasoning provides the necessary insights for these vehicles to act appropriately. This capability not only enhances the safety features of autonomous travel but also contributes to the broader goals of efficiency and sustainability in transportation.

This introduction to spatial reasoning not only sets the stage for exploring how this technology functions within autonomous vehicles but also underscores its transformative impact on the future of mobility. By delving into this subject, we aim to unveil the layers of technology that make autonomous vehicles not just possible, but proficient navigators of our world.

Spatial reasoning in autonomous vehicles is a critical technology that allows these advanced machines to interpret and navigate their environments with high precision. At the heart of this system lies a complex network of sensors, cameras, and radar devices that collect real-time data about the vehicle's surroundings. Each component serves a specific purpose: cameras detect visual cues such as traffic lights and road signs, radars provide velocity data about moving objects, and LIDAR (Light Detection and Ranging) maps out the physical environment with stunning detail using laser light.

The data collected is then processed by highly sophisticated algorithms that form the vehicle's decision-making framework. These algorithms integrate the sensory inputs to create a comprehensive understanding of the surrounding environment. They analyze and interpret this data, similar to how a human driver continually assesses road conditions. For example, if a pedestrian suddenly crosses the road, the system calculates the distance, speed, and trajectory in milliseconds and decides whether to slow down or stop, ensuring safety.

This integration of sensing and intelligent processing allows autonomous vehicles to perform complex navigational tasks, from adjusting the vehicle's path to avoid a pothole to executing safe lane changes on a busy highway.

However, despite its advanced capabilities, spatial reasoning is not without limitations. Factors such as adverse weather conditions or unexpected road scenarios can challenge the accuracy and reliability of sensor data, highlighting the importance of ongoing advancements in sensor technology and algorithmic processing.

By understanding these technical details, one can appreciate the sophisticated orchestration behind an autonomous vehicle's journey, offering insights into both its current capabilities and the potential areas for future enhancement. Such knowledge underscores the importance of spatial reasoning in powering the next generation of transportation solutions, blending intricate technology with practical application for safer and more efficient travel.

Let's take a deeper look at the intricacies of the algorithmic decision-making process in autonomous vehicles, focusing on the integration of various sensory inputs and their real-time responses.

- **Sensor Data Fusion:**
Data from LIDAR, radar, and cameras are crucial for autonomous vehicles to form a comprehensive environmental model. LIDAR provides detailed distance measurements, radar offers velocity data of moving objects, and cameras capture visual information. These different types of data are fused using sophisticated algorithms such as Kalman filters or particle filters, which help in creating a reliable, unified representation of the vehicle's surroundings. This fusion process ensures that the strengths of one type of sensor can compensate for the limitations of another,

resulting in a more accurate environmental model.

- **Decision-Making Algorithms:**

The decision-making process in autonomous vehicles is structured around three core components: object detection, prediction models, and decision trees. Object detection algorithms process the fused sensor data to identify and classify objects such as vehicles, pedestrians, and road signs. Prediction models then anticipate the future movements of these detected objects based on their current states and past behavior. Decision trees evaluate various possible actions the vehicle can take and choose the optimal one based on predefined safety and efficiency criteria. Together, these algorithms allow the vehicle to make informed decisions swiftly and accurately.

- **Error Handling and Redundancy:**

Ensuring reliability in the face of uncertain sensor data or potential algorithmic errors is crucial for safety. Autonomous vehicles incorporate redundancy in both hardware and software to manage errors effectively. Multiple sensors of each type (e.g., several LIDARs or cameras) provide overlapping data streams, allowing the system to cross-verify information and maintain functionality if one sensor fails. Advanced error-checking algorithms detect discrepancies or outliers in sensor data, triggering fallback protocols that can reroute data processing or switch to a safe, minimal-risk driving mode until the issue is resolved.

For instance, imagine an autonomous vehicle approaching a road closure not marked on its map. The vehicle's sensors detect the obstruction, and the fusion algorithm integrates this data to update the vehicle's understanding of the environment. The decision-making algorithms quickly evaluate alternative routes while considering the movement of nearby vehicles and pedestrians. If there's conflicting data or an unclear path, the system engages error-handling protocols to either find a safe path through or stop the vehicle entirely until more reliable data is available, ensuring safety despite the unexpected challenge.

These detailed processes underline the complexity and sophistication behind the decision-making in autonomous vehicles, showcasing a perfect blend of advanced technology and practical application, all designed to deliver safer, more efficient autonomous driving.

In autonomous vehicles, the synthesis of data from LIDAR, radar, and cameras forms the bedrock of spatial reasoning, enabling these vehicles to interpret and interact with their environment intelligently. LIDAR, which stands for Light Detection and Ranging, uses laser beams to create high-resolution maps of the vehicle's surroundings by measuring how long it takes for the light to return after hitting an object. This technology provides precise distance measurements and a detailed 3D view of the environment.

Radar complements LIDAR by using radio waves to detect objects and gauge their speed and direction. This is especially useful in harsh weather conditions like fog or heavy rain, where optical devices like cameras and LIDAR may be less effective. Cameras add another layer of data, capturing visual details such as road signs, traffic lights, and lane markings.

Artificial Intelligence (AI) plays a crucial role in processing and interpreting this multi-sensor data. The integration process, known as sensor fusion, involves AI algorithms that combine the different data streams to form a coherent model of the vehicle's surroundings. These algorithms are trained to recognize patterns and make contextual sense of the diverse data collected. For example, while LIDAR might detect an object's shape and radar its velocity, the camera might help identify it as a pedestrian.

Once the data is fused, AI uses it for spatial reasoning—understanding the vehicle's position relative to other objects and making predictive assessments that guide decision-making. This might include calculating the safest path, adjusting speed, or preparing for potential hazards like a pedestrian stepping into the road. Each decision is based on a comprehensive analysis of the integrated data, ensuring that actions taken are informed and contextually appropriate.

Highlighting both the sophistication of these technologies and their potential limitations—such as dependency on clear weather conditions for optimal sensor performance—provides a realistic appreciation of current capabilities and areas ripe for future development. The integration of LIDAR, radar, and cameras, interpreted through advanced AI, not only exemplifies high-tech engineering but also illustrates a critical step towards fully autonomous and safer transportation systems. This intricate dance of technology is what moves autonomous vehicles beyond mere machines to perceptive entities capable of navigating our complex world.

1. Data Collection:
LIDAR sensors on autonomous vehicles emit laser beams to measure the distance to various objects, creating a detailed 3D map of the environment. Radar sensors use radio waves to detect objects and calculate their speed and direction, offering robust data even under poor visibility conditions such as fog or heavy rain. Concurrently, cameras capture high-resolution images providing rich visual information about the environment including road signs, traffic signals, and lane markers. Each sensor type is pivotal, gathering unique data that, when combined, offers a comprehensive view of surrounding conditions.

2. Data Preprocessing:
Before integration, raw data from each type of sensor undergoes preprocessing to ensure standardization and accuracy. This includes normalization of scale and resolution, alignment of timestamp references, and calibration of sensor outputs. Noise reduction techniques, such as filtering and smoothing algorithms, are applied to eliminate sensor noise and correct data errors. Faulty or outlier data points identified during this phase are managed through error-handling protocols, ensuring only reliable data progresses to the fusion stage.

3. Sensor Fusion Algorithms:
The fusion of data from LIDAR, radar, and cameras is achieved through sophisticated algorithms. Kalman Filters are often employed to dynamically merge data in a

statistically optimal way. Neural Networks could be utilized to enhance the fusion process with learning capabilities that can improve data integration over time:

```
pseudo
function fuseData(lidarData, radarData, cameraData):
    fusedData = initializeFusionModel()
    for data in [lidarData, radarData, cameraData]:
        if NeuralNetwork.isApplicable():
            fusedData    =    NeuralNetwork.integrate(data,
fusedData)
        else:
            fusedData    =    KalmanFilter.combine(data,
fusedData)
    return fusedData
```

These algorithms weigh data based on reliability and relevance, constructing a unified environmental model that continuously updates as new sensor input is received.

4. Decision-Making Process:

Utilizing the fused environmental model, the vehicle's AI engages in complex spatial reasoning to navigate safely. Object recognition algorithms identify and classify objects such as vehicles, pedestrians, and obstacles. Path planning modules compute the best routes while considering potential hazards and traffic conditions. AI-driven decision systems analyze these elements to make real-time decisions like adjusting vehicle speed, planning lane changes, or initiating emergency brakes:

```
pseudo
if detectEmergency(fusedData):
    executeEmergencyBraking()
```

```
else:
    path = calculateOptimalPath(fusedData)
    executeManeuvers(path)
```

This decision-making pipeline ensures responsive and adaptable navigation tailored to real-word driving scenarios.

5. Feedback Loop:

A continuous feedback loop enhances system performance where real-time data from vehicle operations feedback into the sensor fusion and decision algorithms. This feedback mechanism allows for ongoing adjustments and learning, refining both the accuracy of the sensor fusion and the effectiveness of decision-making processes over time. Calibration updates, machine learning adaptations, and refined algorithms contribute to this self-improving system, closing the loop on an intelligent, learning-driven operation system.

Through these detailed stages, the complex orchestration behind autonomous driving systems illuminates the thorough technological integration required for effective, safe autonomous travel. This breakdown not only showcases the practical applications but also emphasizes the continued advancements necessary to keep pushing the boundaries of what these incredible machines can do.

Imagine you're a conductor orchestrating a symphony, where every musician must play in perfect harmony. This is not unlike what the Waymo project and Tesla's Autopilot system achieve with spatial reasoning in the realm of autonomous vehicles. Each sensor and piece of technology operates in concert to navigate roads with precision and awareness, akin to a well-trained orchestra responding to its conductor's cues.

Take Waymo, for example, which integrates a variety of sensors like LIDAR, cameras, and radar to create a detailed understanding of its environment. Think of it as attending a dinner party where you're trying to listen to multiple conversations at once. Waymo's technology allows the vehicle to 'listen'—or in this case, 'sense'—everything around it, combining these inputs to make safe driving decisions. This seamless integration helps it navigate complex urban environments where interpreting vast amounts of data quickly is crucial.

Then, there's Tesla's Autopilot, akin to a seasoned chess player who's anticipating their opponent's next several moves. It uses cameras primarily to understand its surroundings and make instant decisions, from changing lanes on a highway to adjusting speeds based on the traffic flow. This system continually learns from its experiences, improving its responses over time, much like a chess player refining their strategy throughout a tournament.

Both systems showcase the power of spatial reasoning by not just reacting to their immediate surroundings but by anticipating and planning several moves ahead. This capability is crucial not only for safety but for enhancing the overall driving experience—turning what used to be a hands-on task into one where the car does the thinking for you.

These examples illuminate the intricate dance between various technologies that enable autonomous vehicles to navigate our complex, ever-changing world, offering a glimpse into a future where cars are more than just machines; they're intuitive, intelligent companions on the road.

Here is a breakdown of how Tesla's Autopilot and Waymo's driving systems integrate and use sensor data for decision-making. This detailed exploration aims to provide clarity on the technological underpinnings that allow these systems to operate efficiently and safely.

Sensor Integration in Waymo:
- **Types of Sensors Used:**
  - **LIDAR:** Utilizes light in the form of a pulsed laser to measure variable distances to the earth, creating precise 3D information about the shape of the surrounding environment.
  - **Radar:** Employs radio waves to detect the distance and speed of objects, particularly effective under varied weather conditions.
  - **Cameras:** Capture high-resolution images providing crucial visual detail, facilitating object and sign recognition.

- **Data Processing:**
  - **Integration Techniques:** Data from LIDAR, radar, and cameras are fused using complex algorithms to create a coherent, comprehensive model of the surroundings.
  - **Analysis:** Advanced machine learning techniques are applied to interpret the fused data, identifying relevant objects, predicting actions of pedestrians, and other vehicles.

- **Decision Algorithms:**

   - **Path Planning Algorithms:** These algorithms calculate the optimal path and maneuvers based on the processed data, considering factors like obstacles, lane constraints, and traffic laws.

   - **Behavior Prediction:** By anticipating the actions of other traffic participators, Waymo can make proactive adjustments to its driving strategy, enhancing safety and flow.

Tesla Autopilot's Functionality:
- Primary Sensing Technology:
   - **Cameras:** Tesla's system is heavily reliant on camera input, which captures and interprets visual data for real-time decision-making, similar to the human visual system.

- Software and Algorithms:
   - **Computer Vision Algorithms:** These algorithms analyze the camera feeds to detect lane markings, read road signs, and observe nearby traffic participants.

   - **Autosteer and Auto Lane Change:** Utilizes the processed visual data to keep the vehicle within its lane and perform necessary lane changes safely.

- Learning Mechanism:
   - **Neural Networks:** Tesla's neural networks learn from vast amounts of driving data, enhancing their decision-making capabilities over time.

   - **Continuous Learning:** The system evolves by continuously analyzing driving situations and outcomes, refining its algorithms based on real-world feedback to improve future performance.

Through this detailed examination, the intricate orchestra

of sensors, software, and advanced algorithms that power both Waymo and Tesla's autonomous driving capabilities become clear. Understanding these components elucidates how these vehicles interpret their environments and make informed decisions, ensuring their operation is as safe and effective as human driving, if not more so. This depth of technological integration not only showcases the potential of autonomous vehicles but also emphasizes the continuous advancements that push the boundaries of modern transportation.

Autonomous vehicles rely on sophisticated spatial reasoning capabilities to navigate safely, yet they face several significant challenges, including sensor reliability, data interpretation errors, and regulatory hurdles. Each of these components plays a crucial role in how effectively these vehicles operate in real-world scenarios, and understanding these factors is essential for appreciating the current state and future potential of autonomous driving technology.

Sensor Reliability:

Sensors like LIDAR, radar, and cameras are the eyes and ears of autonomous vehicles, tasked with gathering critical data about the vehicle's surroundings. However, these sensors can sometimes fail or deliver inaccurate information due to various factors such as adverse weather conditions, sensor misalignment, or unexpected obstructions. For instance, heavy rain or fog can severely impair a sensor's ability to detect nearby objects, much like how a human driver might struggle to see the road in poor weather conditions.

Data Interpretation Errors:

Once data is collected, it must be accurately interpreted—a process that is not always straightforward. Interpretation errors can occur, leading to misjudgments about the vehicle's environment. These errors might be due to flaws in the algorithms processing the sensor data or unexpected scenarios that the vehicle's AI has not been trained to handle. Consider a scenario where an autonomous vehicle misinterprets a harmless roadside banner as a moving vehicle due to fluttering in the wind. Such misinterpretations could lead to unnecessary or incorrect driving maneuvers, compromising safety.

Regulatory Hurdles:

Navigating the regulatory landscape presents another layer of complexity. Regulations governing autonomous vehicles vary widely across different regions and are continually evolving. Manufacturers must ensure their vehicles comply with diverse and changing regulations, which can impede rapid deployment and testing. Moreover, there's the need for standardized protocols for how vehicles report accidents or share data with regulatory bodies, similar to how aviation has strict reporting and operational guidelines.

Understanding these challenges highlights both the sophistication of the technology driving autonomous vehicles and the hurdles that need to be overcome. As the industry addresses these issues, the path forward includes improving sensor technologies, refining data processing algorithms, and working with regulatory bodies to establish clear guidelines. This concerted effort will further integrate autonomous vehicles into everyday life, improving their reliability and safety for all road users. They are not just vehicles; they represent a pivotal shift in how transportation systems integrate with urban environments and technology.

Let's take a deeper look at how regulatory hurdles influence the deployment and testing of autonomous vehicles, offering insight into the complex landscape of rules that govern this cutting-edge technology.

- **Regulatory Requirements**:
- **Safety Standards**: Autonomous vehicles are required to meet rigorous safety standards that ensure they can operate as safely as human drivers. This includes crashworthiness standards, system reliability assessments, and performance benchmarks during various driving conditions.
- **Data Privacy Laws**: Given the large amounts of data these vehicles collect, manufacturers must comply with data protection laws such as GDPR in Europe or CCPA in California, which dictate how data is collected, stored, and shared.
- **Interoperability Requirements**: These regulations ensure that different systems and components within autonomous vehicles can work together seamlessly and also integrate safely with public infrastructure like traffic signals and road sensors.

- **Regional Variations**:
- **United States**: The U.S. has a mixed regulatory approach where both federal and state regulations apply, leading to a patchwork of laws that can vary significantly

from one state to another.

- **European Union**: The EU tends to have more uniform regulations across its member states, focusing heavily on privacy and safety through directives and regulations that all member states must follow.

- **Asia**: Countries like Japan and South Korea are rapidly developing their regulatory frameworks to support the deployment of autonomous vehicles, with a strong focus on integrating advanced technology with public transportation systems.

- **Compliance Strategies**:

- Companies like Waymo and Tesla engage continuously with regulatory bodies to shape and respond to new regulations. This includes providing data from test drives, participating in public hearings, and being part of advisory groups.

- Participation in pilot programs allows these companies to deploy their vehicles in real-world scenarios under regulatory supervision, providing crucial data that informs both policy and product development.

- Implementation of advanced compliance management systems ensures that all aspects of vehicle design and operation are in line with current laws and standards, dynamically adjusting to changes as needed.

- **Impact on Innovation**:

- While necessary for public safety and confidence, stringent regulations can also slow down technological advancement. For instance, the slow pace of law updates can lag behind technological capabilities, delaying the introduction of potentially life-saving innovations.

- On the other hand, clear and thoughtful regulations can spur innovation by setting guidelines that promote safety without stifling creativity, as seen in the proactive regulatory approaches of countries like Singapore.

This detailed exploration shows that while regulatory frameworks present significant challenges, they are also pivotal in shaping the safe and effective integration of autonomous vehicles into our daily lives. By navigating these regulations wisely, companies can not only comply with current requirements but also drive forward the innovation that will define the future of transportation.

The future of spatial reasoning in autonomous vehicles points towards significant advancements in both sensor technology and AI algorithms, which are anticipated to dramatically enhance the precision and efficacy of these systems. As we advance, sensor technology will likely grow more sophisticated with developments that may include higher resolution LIDAR sensors and more sensitive radar systems. These advancements would enable vehicles not only to detect obstacles with greater accuracy but also to discern finer details in the environment around them, such as small road debris or subtleties in road surface conditions.

Parallel to improvements in hardware, advancements in AI algorithms will play a critical role in spatial reasoning. Future algorithms are expected to be more robust in their decision-making capabilities, incorporating deeper learning techniques that allow them to predict and react to dynamic road scenarios with unprecedented accuracy. These algorithms will likely use vast datasets to improve their predictive capabilities, learning from a wider array of driving conditions and scenarios to function effectively across different global regions with distinct traffic rules and patterns.

Moreover, the integration of AI with enhanced sensor technology could lead to vehicles that understand not just the physical world but also the intentions of other road users. For example, advanced AI may predict a pedestrian's movements not merely based on their current speed and trajectory but by analyzing body language and eye contact. This level of interpretative capability could revolutionize how safely and smoothly autonomous vehicles navigate through crowded urban spaces.

Additionally, as regulations evolve to keep pace with technological innovations, there could be a synergistic effect whereby clearer regulatory frameworks catalyze further technological advancements. This supportive cycle would not only accelerate the development of autonomous vehicles but also bolster public trust and acceptance of these technologies.

In essence, the advancements in spatial reasoning and the resulting improvements in autonomous vehicle technologies are set to transform our transportation systems dramatically. Such technologies promise not only enhanced safety and efficiency but also a redefinition of the vehicular experience, shaping a future where vehicles are not mere conveyances but intelligent, aware participants in the broader spectrum of urban life.

Let's take a deeper look at how emerging sensor technologies and advanced AI algorithms are poised to transform the spatial reasoning capabilities of autonomous vehicles.

Sensor Technologies:
- Varieties and Specifications:
- **Next-Generation LIDAR:** Future LIDAR sensors are expected to offer increased range and resolution, allowing vehicles to detect objects from greater distances and with higher detail, crucial for complex urban environments.
- **Enhanced Sensitivity Radar:** Improvements in radar technology may include better sensitivity and object differentiation, which can drastically improve the vehicle's ability to navigate in adverse weather conditions like fog or heavy rain.
- **High-Definition Cameras:** Cameras will likely evolve to capture images at higher definitions, providing richer visual data which aids in better object and sign recognition.

- Functionality Enhancements:
- **Range and Resolution:** Future sensors will boast extended ranges and finer resolutions. This enhancement means that autonomous vehicles can detect smaller objects, such as debris on the road, from further away, giving the AI more time to make informed decisions.
- **Speed of Data Processing:** With improvements in sensor technology, the speed at which data is processed will increase, allowing for near-instantaneous responses to changing road conditions.

AI Algorithm Enhancements:
- Algorithm Types:
- **Deep Learning Models:** These models will become more sophisticated, enabling them to learn from vast amounts of data more efficiently, leading to improved accuracy in object detection and event prediction.
- **Real-Time Decision-Making Systems:** These systems will use incoming sensor data to make immediate driving decisions, crucial for ensuring safety in dynamic driving environments.

- Capabilities:
- **Predictive Analytics:** Advanced AI will incorporate predictive analytics that take into account a wide array of possible road conditions and driver behaviors, thereby enhancing the ability to foresee and react to potential hazards before they pose a threat.

Integration Techniques:
- Data Fusion Methods:
- **Advanced Sensor Fusion:** Future development will focus on creating more sophisticated methods for integrating data from various sensors, possibly using neural networks or machine learning to weigh and merge data more effectively, producing a more accurate and comprehensive view of the vehicle's surroundings.

- Application Examples:
- **Interpreting Pedestrian Intent:** Advanced AI might analyze the speed, trajectory, and even body language of

pedestrians to determine their intent, allowing vehicles to anticipate and react to potential jaywalkers or other irregular pedestrian movements.

- **Navigating Complex Environments:** In urban settings filled with a multitude of stimuli, the integrated data can help vehicles make smarter route choices, avoid unexpected obstacles, and interact safely with other road users.

This exploration into the integration of advanced sensor technologies and AI algorithms highlights how autonomous vehicles are evolving into more intuitive and capable systems. These advancements not only promise enhanced safety and efficiency but also pave the way for a future where vehicles interact seamlessly with their environments, much like an experienced driver.

Spatial reasoning is fundamentally transforming the landscape of autonomous vehicles by dramatically enhancing their ability to navigate complex environments safely and efficiently. This capability enables vehicles to interpret vast amounts of sensory data in real time, calculating distances, identifying objects, and predicting the movements of other road users. Such comprehensive environmental awareness significantly reduces the risk of accidents, positioning spatial reasoning as a critical component in the pursuit of safer roads.

Moreover, spatial reasoning optimizes routes and traffic management, contributing to increased travel efficiency. It allows autonomous vehicles to adjust their speed, plan optimal paths, and react promptly to unexpected changes in their surroundings, such as sudden traffic jams or detours. This not only helps in conserving energy by ensuring smoother rides but also reduces traffic congestion, ultimately minimizing the environmental footprint of daily commutes.

The impact of spatial reasoning extends beyond merely navigating physical obstacles; it plays a pivotal role in how autonomous vehicles coexist with human-driven vehicles, creating a cohesive flow of heterogeneous traffic. This integration promises a future where transportation is not only autonomous but also inherently connected, making travel more reliable and systematic. As this technology continues to evolve and integrate deeper into urban infrastructures, it envisions a new era of transportation that emphasizes safety, efficiency, and sustainability.

AI IN SPATIAL DATA HANDLING

Artificial intelligence is significantly transforming the field of spatial data handling, introducing unprecedented efficiency and accuracy to systems traditionally bogged down by the complexity and volume of the data processed. At its core, AI enhances the capabilities of Geographic Information Systems (GIS) and remote sensing, technologies that play vital roles in everything from urban planning to environmental monitoring. By integrating AI, these systems can now handle and interpret vast arrays of spatial data more swiftly and with greater precision than ever before.

The strength of AI in this domain lies in its ability to quickly analyze and learn from the data, identifying patterns and insights that would be invisible or time-consuming for human analysts to discern. This capability not only speeds up the process of data handling but also improves the quality of the decisions and predictions made from this data. For instance, city planners can utilize AI-driven insights to optimize everything from traffic flow to disaster response strategies, enhancing both the safety and quality of urban living.

This chapter explores how AI is revolutionized spatial data handling, delving into specific applications within GIS and remote sensing, and discussing the broader implications of these advancements. Each section is designed to build upon the last, gradually unfolding the sophisticated interplay between AI technologies and spatial data to provide a comprehensive understanding of this dynamic field. With this foundation, we aim to not just inform but also inspire a deeper appreciation of how AI-driven technologies are reshaping our approach to managing the spaces we live in and the environments we wish to preserve.

Spatial data, essentially the digital information about the location, shape, and size of physical objects on Earth, forms the foundation of Geographic Information Systems (GIS) and other mapping technologies. It is distinctive because it connects physical locations to descriptive information, creating layers that are inherently more complex than mere numerical or textual data. This complexity presents unique challenges in processing effectively, primarily due to the volume, variety, and the dynamic nature of the data involved.

One primary difficulty in handling spatial data effectively is its sheer volume. As technology advances, the amount of data collected from satellites, aerial drones, and ground-based sensors continues to grow exponentially. Managing and processing this vast quantity of data requires significant computational resources and sophisticated algorithms, demanding more from traditional database and software systems.

Moreover, the variety of spatial data, from raw satellite images to intricate 3D models, adds another layer of complexity. Each type of data may require different processing techniques and tools, making standardization a challenge. For instance, the way data is captured in urban mapping - high-resolution images identifying road networks and building outlines - vastly differs from ecological mapping which may rely more on landscape patterns and vegetation data.

Another issue is accuracy and precision. Spatial data must be extremely precise to be useful in most applications, particularly in fields like urban planning or disaster management. Inaccuracies in GPS data or image resolution can lead to ineffective or even hazardous decisions, like poorly designed evacuation routes in crisis situations.

Furthermore, the dynamic nature of spatial data means that it constantly changes. Roads, landscapes, and urban structures are not static; they evolve, and so must the data that represents them. Ensuring that spatial databases are up-to-date is a daunting task, particularly when dealing with areas undergoing rapid development or natural changes.

Given these complexities, traditional methods often fall short, struggling with inefficiencies that AI and machine learning technologies are increasingly equipped to overcome. By applying AI, patterns can be extracted faster from massive datasets, predictions can be made with greater accuracy, and real-time data updates can be integrated smoothly, transforming spatial data handling into a more efficient and scalable endeavor.

Let's take a detailed look at the sophisticated algorithms that power AI for spatial data analysis, focusing on how they streamline processing and manage dynamic data efficiently.

- **Types of Algorithms**:
- **Convolutional Neural Networks (CNNs)**: Often used for image recognition tasks, CNNs are crucial in analyzing and interpreting spatial data from aerial and satellite imagery. They effectively identify patterns and features such as road networks, building footprints, and natural landscapes.
- **Recurrent Neural Networks (RNNs)**: Perfect for dealing with time series data, RNNs play a significant role in predicting changes over time in spatial environments. They can forecast future conditions based on historical data, essential for urban planning and disaster management.
- **Graphic Processing Units (GPUs)**: These are specialized electronic circuits designed to rapidly manipulate and alter memory to accelerate the creation of images in a frame buffer intended for output to a display device. GPUs are very efficient at manipulating computer graphics and image processing.

- **Data Processing**:
- **Data Cleaning**: AI algorithms first clean the gathered spatial data, which involves removing inaccuracies and correcting any form of data anomalies.
- **Data Integration**: Various sources of spatial data are integrated. AI uses algorithms to synchronize data from different sources, ensuring consistency across datasets.
- **Data Transformation**: Before analysis, data transformation is performed to convert raw data into a format that is more appropriate for making predictions. This step is crucial for enhancing the accuracy of the models employed.

- **Real-time Data Handling**:
  - **Incremental Learning**: This technique allows AI models to learn continuously from new data without forgetting their existing knowledge. It's particularly useful in environments where spatial configurations frequently change.
  - **Continuous Data Stream Processing**: AI systems use algorithms that can process and analyze data streams in real time. This ability is essential for applications that require immediate response, such as traffic management systems and emergency response during natural disasters.

- **Application Scenarios**:
  - **Urban Infrastructure Adjustment**: In rapidly growing cities, AI-driven spatial analysis helps urban planners to optimize infrastructure layouts, predict traffic patterns, and plan public transportation routes efficiently.
  - **Evacuation Route Planning**: During emergencies, AI models quickly analyze the current situation to update and optimize evacuation routes, helping to clear areas faster and save lives by predicting hazardous zones in real time.

These AI innovations demonstrate not only a capacity to handle complex spatial data but also an ability to enhance decision-making in critical, dynamic settings. By leveraging these advanced technologies, professionals can respond more adeptly to changing environmental conditions and societal needs, leading to smarter, more sustainable development and improved safety measures.

Imagine artificial intelligence in Geographic Information

Systems (GIS) as the brainy conductor of a grand orchestra, where every musician represents a piece of geographical data. Just as the conductor effortlessly reads and interprets the complex scores, cueing in various instruments to create beautiful harmony, AI in GIS expertly manages and analyzes extensive geographical data. This technology sifts through layers upon layers of maps and datasets—much like a conductor oversees strings, woodwinds, brass, and percussion—ensuring all elements come together perfectly to compose the most accurate and useful interpretation of the geographic landscape.

In this role, AI scans the immense volumes of data, much like a conductor listens to each note. It identifies patterns and connections that might go unnoticed to the unaided eye, such as subtle changes in land usage over time or predicting areas at greater risk for flooding. The process isn't just about handling data efficiently; it's about making this information truly useful, turning raw data into a comprehensive geographical narrative that city planners, conservationists, and many others can rely upon to make informed decisions.

Just as a skilled conductor makes adjustments in real-time to harmonize the orchestra's output, AI dynamically refines its data analyses based on the latest information, ensuring the interpretations remain timely and relevant. It's a continuous, fluid process that helps navigate the complexities of our ever-changing physical world, making AI an indispensable maestro in the realm of GIS, orchestrating data into decisions that shape everything from urban development to environmental conservation.

Artificial intelligence significantly enhances the capabilities of remote sensing, a technology that utilizes satellites or aircraft to collect data about the Earth without direct contact. Traditionally, interpreting these vast streams of data from space required extensive time and was prone to human error. With AI, the process becomes more refined, fast, and accurate, enabling the detection of subtle environmental changes with unprecedented precision.

AI conducts this by employing sophisticated algorithms to analyze the raw data captured by remote sensors. It starts by filtering out noise or irrelevant information, much like a photographer adjusting a lens to capture a sharper image. These algorithms can pinpoint changes in vegetation, water bodies, urban expansion, and more by processing different wavelengths of light reflected from the Earth's surface that human eyes cannot see.

Once AI identifies these changes, it categorizes and quantifies them, allowing for detailed monitoring over time. For example, AI can detect slight alterations in forest health indicators or coastal erosion, providing early warnings for potential ecological crises. This aspect is crucial for environmental monitoring, disaster response, and urban planning, offering a level of detail that manual methods cannot match.

Moreover, AI adapts and learns from new data, continuously improving its analysis. This attribute means that the more it processes, the better it becomes at predicting future changes, thereby not just acting as a passive observer but a proactive predictor.

As AI in remote sensing evolves, it faces challenges such as dealing with cloud cover or differentiating between natural and human-made changes. However, the ongoing advancements in machine learning and data processing are gradually overcoming these hurdles, paving the way for more robust and insightful environmental monitoring from space. This integration of AI promises to turn satellite imagery into a dynamic tool for global awareness and timely intervention, marking a significant leap forward in how we understand and interact with our planet.

Remote sensing technology employs a variety of sophisticated AI algorithms to interpret satellite imagery effectively. This section breaks down the types of algorithms used, their specific applications in noise reduction, the learning mechanisms that enhance their efficiency, and real-world environmental monitoring scenarios.

1. **Types of Algorithms:**
   - **Convolutional Neural Networks (CNNs)**: These are particularly effective for image classification and analysis tasks because they can automatically detect important features without any human supervision. In the context of satellite imagery, CNNs can identify and classify various environmental features such as water bodies, forest cover, and urban areas.
   - **Support Vector Machines (SVMs)**: SVMs are useful for classification and regression challenges. They work well for remote sensing as they help in accurately classifying land cover types in satellite images, even when the data is not

linearly separable.

2. **Noise Reduction Techniques:**
- **Fourier Transforms**: This mathematical technique transforms the satellite image data from the time domain to the frequency domain, helping to identify and filter out recurring noise patterns, such as atmospheric disturbances.
- **Spectral Analysis**: This involves examining the various wavelengths of light reflected from the Earth to detect disturbances or anomalies in satellite imagery, effectively reducing noise and enhancing the clarity of the data.

3. **Learning Mechanisms:**
- **Supervised Learning**: This method involves training an algorithm on a labeled dataset, which is particularly useful in remote sensing for classifying land cover or detecting specific changes over time when prior labeled instances are available.
- **Unsupervised Learning**: Useful in clustering similar data points together, such as grouping different types of terrain or natural features without prior labeling.
- **Reinforcement Learning**: Although less common in traditional remote sensing, this technique can be used in dynamic environments where the algorithm learns to make decisions based on the rewards or feedback it receives from changes in environmental conditions.

4. **Real-World Application Examples:**
- **Monitoring Deforestation Rates in the Amazon**: Using CNNs, algorithms can analyze time-lapsed images to

detect changes in forest density, providing insights into the rate and localization of deforestation activities.

- **Tracking Urban Sprawl in Major Cities**: SVMs can help in classifying urban, suburban, and rural areas by analyzing the spread and development patterns in satellite images over several years.

These algorithms not only streamline the processing of vast amounts of satellite data but also enhance the accuracy and timeliness of environmental monitoring. By continually adapting and learning from new data, these AI systems provide crucial insights enabling better decision-making for environmental preservation and urban planning.

Imagine artificial intelligence (AI) in the world of spatial data handling as akin to a highly skilled data analyst, one endowed not only with remarkable speed but also an unmatched precision in sifting through mountains of complex data. Consider a massive library filled to the brim with books where each page contains bits of crucial yet raw data. Just like a seasoned librarian who knows exactly where every piece of information is stored and how to swiftly retrieve it, AI streamlines the process of navigating through this immense volume of spatial data.

AI does not merely scan through the data; it dissects and understands each layer, akin to how our expert would extract key narratives from a pile of disorganized documents. For instance, in processing satellite images to monitor environmental changes, AI would rapidly identify and categorize changes in vegetation, water bodies, or urban expansion in much the same way a detective pieces together clues to solve a complex case swiftly and efficiently.

This capability transforms raw data into actionable insights, much like how our hypothetical analyst could quickly pull reports that influence critical business decisions. The impact of AI in this scenario isn't just about the speed or ease of data handling but about its ability to empower decision-makers in real time, ensuring that interventions are timely, policies are relevant, and developmental impacts are maximized.

By embracing this transformative tool, the field of spatial data handling moves from mere data collection to being a cornerstone of informed decision making in urban planning, environmental protection, and beyond, marking a significant evolution in how we interact with and manage our physical surroundings.

Here is a detailed breakdown of the specific AI technologies used in spatial data handling, designed to offer a clear and practical explanation of how each component functions and its impact on managing spatial data effectively:

- **Types of AI Technologies:**
  - **Machine Learning Algorithms:**
    - **Supervised Learning:** Utilized for pattern recognition in satellite imagery, this algorithm trains on labeled data to classify land cover or detect changes over time.
    - **Unsupervised Learning:** Ideal for categorizing new data without predefined labels, this method is used to

identify clusters or patterns in spatial data, such as differentiating natural landscapes based on vegetation types.

- **Neural Networks:**
- **Convolutional Neural Networks (CNNs):** These networks perform exceptionally well in image processing, essential for analyzing spatial data from aerial photography and satellite imagery. They automatically detect important features like roads, buildings, and rivers without human supervision.

- **Data Processing Techniques:**
- **Data Cleaning:**
- **Noise Reduction:** Techniques like smoothing and filtering are used to remove statistical noise from data, ensuring the accuracy of the analyses.
- **Error Correction:** Algorithms detect and correct errors in the data, such as inaccuracies in GPS coordinates or misalignment in multi-temporal datasets.
- **Data Integration:**
- **Source Synchronization:** AI integrates spatial data from disparate sources, aligning different datasets to a uniform coordinate system for consistent analysis.
- **Accuracy Checks:** AI systems validate the integrated data against known benchmarks or through cross-referencing to enhance reliability and accuracy.

- **Real-Time Analysis Capabilities:**
- **Streaming Data Analysis:**
- **Immediate Processing:** AI analyzes incoming data streams in real-time, crucial for applications like disaster response where timely information is paramount.
- **Predictive Analytics:**

- **Forecasting Models:** AI uses historical data to predict future scenarios, such as projecting urban growth or anticipating natural events like floods or wildfires, aiding in preemptive planning and resource management.

- **Impact on Decision-Making:**
- **Policy Development:**
- **Environmental Conservation:** AI-driven insights help formulate policies on land use, conservation strategies, and environmental monitoring protocols.
- **Urban Planning:** AI analyzes spatial data to inform the development of infrastructure, optimizing everything from public transportation routes to zoning regulations.
- **Operational Efficiency:**
- **Speed and Accuracy:** By automating the data analysis process, AI drastically reduces the time needed to derive insights from spatial data and increases decision-making precision, leading to more effective management and implementation of plans.

This comprehensive exploration highlights how advanced AI technologies seamlessly integrate into the frameworks of spatial data handling, illuminating their pivotal roles in enhancing efficiency, accuracy, and functionality in various sectors reliant on geographical data.

Jack Dangermond, the founder of Esri, has had a transformative impact on urban planning through the innovative use of Geographic Information Systems (GIS). Esri's tools, powered significantly by artificial intelligence (AI), play a crucial role in modernizing and enhancing urban planning processes. These tools take complex spatial data and transform it into digestible, actionable insights that urban planners and decision-makers can utilize efficiently and effectively.

The cornerstone of this transformation is the integration of AI with the ArcGIS platform. AI in ArcGIS facilitates the analysis of large datasets that describe cities in high detail—from demographic distributions and traffic patterns to environmental conditions and infrastructure networks. This integration allows urban planners to not only visualize but also simulate the effects of potential changes in urban environments.

For instance, Esri's AI capabilities enable predictive modeling, which predicts urban growth patterns, assesses risk, and anticipates future demands on public services and infrastructure. This function is paramount in planning for sustainable city development, as it assists in understanding how today's decisions will impact tomorrow's urban landscapes.

Moreover, AI-driven spatial analytics in ArcGIS complements traditional urban planning techniques by providing tools such as scenario planning and real-time data analysis. Planners can now forecast scenarios involving population growth, natural disasters, and changing land uses with a degree of precision previously unattainable. They can also receive immediate feedback on the effectiveness of certain policies or projects, enabling a more adaptive approach to urban management.

The systematic integration of AI by Esri under Dangermond's guidance has not only optimized existing processes but has also opened new avenues for innovation in urban planning. This is achieved by fostering a deeper understanding of complex urban systems in a way that is both accessible and comprehensive, ensuring urban environments are more livable, resilient, and sustainable. Thus, Dangermond's contributions extend beyond technical advancements, influencing a fundamental shift in how cities are planned and managed for the betterment of their inhabitants.

Integrating artificial intelligence (AI) into spatial data analysis presents several significant challenges, ranging from technical limitations to ethical dilemmas. These challenges require careful consideration and innovative solutions to ensure the effective and responsible use of AI in this field.

One major technical obstacle is the quality and quantity of data required for robust AI analysis. Spatial datasets are often massive and complex, with varied accuracy and resolution. Ensuring the consistency and cleanliness of this data is crucial, as AI systems depend heavily on the quality of input data to produce reliable outputs. This issue is being addressed by developing more sophisticated data preprocessing techniques that enhance data integrity and usability.

Another challenge lies in the computational demands of processing extensive spatial datasets. The sheer volume of data can overwhelm traditional computing infrastructures. To combat this, experts are increasingly turning to cloud computing solutions and specialized hardware that can handle large-scale data operations more efficiently.

From an ethical standpoint, concerns about privacy and data security are paramount, especially when handling geospatial data that can be sensitive or personally identifiable. Ensuring that AI systems comply with data protection laws and ethical guidelines is critical. Experts are tackling these issues by implementing stringent data governance frameworks and using advanced encryption methods to secure data.

Additionally, there is the risk of bias in AI algorithms, where the system might develop skewed insights based on flawed or biased input data. This can lead to unfair or inaccurate spatial analysis outcomes. Researchers and practitioners are addressing this challenge by diversifying training datasets and developing algorithms that can detect and correct bias autonomously.

Through these concerted efforts, the integration of AI into spatial data analysis is advancing, overcoming obstacles to unlock new potentials in urban planning, environmental monitoring, and beyond. This progression not only improves the analytical capabilities but also fosters a deeper understanding and more thoughtful implementation of AI in managing our physical spaces.

Let's take a closer look at the various preprocessing techniques, computational solutions, and bias detection mechanisms utilized in AI for enhancing spatial data analysis.

- **Preprocessing Techniques:**
- **Data Normalization:** In spatial data analysis, normalization is crucial for standardizing the range of data features. This process adjusts the scale of input variables so that they fit within a specific range, like 0 to 1 or -1 to 1, which helps in preventing data dominance (where one variable overshadows others because of differing units or scales). This standardization ensures more stable and faster convergence during the learning phase of AI models.
- **Data Transformation:** Techniques such as logarithmic transformation or square root transformation play a significant role in stabilizing variance and making the data distribution more symmetrical. For instance, if the data is heavily skewed, applying a log transformation can reduce the effect of outliers, thereby normalizing the distribution.
- **Handling Missing Values:** Missing values in spatial data can lead to inaccurate models and biased analysis. Imputation strategies are employed to address this by replacing missing data with statistical estimates like the mean, median, or mode of the column, depending on which metric best suits the data's characteristics. Another approach is predictive imputation, where models like k-NN or regression are used to estimate missing values based on known part of the data.

- **Computational Solutions:**
- **Cloud Computing:** Cloud platforms fundamentally change how large datasets are processed, providing scalable and flexible resources that can be adjusted according to the project's demand. This capability allows spatial data analysts

to handle large datasets more efficiently without investing in expensive infrastructure. Cloud services also facilitate collaborative AI model training and deployment across various locations.

- **Specialized Hardware:** GPUs (Graphics Processing Units) and TPUs (Tensor Processing Units) are at the forefront of processing large-scale spatial datasets. GPUs accelerate the operations of matrix mathematics essential for deep learning models, while TPUs are designed to further speed up tensor manipulations crucial for neural network computations, enhancing the overall efficiency of large-model training and inference.

- **Bias Detection in AI Algorithms:**

- **Algorithm Types:** Fairness-aware machine learning algorithms are specifically designed to detect and mitigate biases that can occur in AI model predictions. These algorithms incorporate techniques to adjust the decision boundaries or weights of models to compensate for known biases in the training data.

- **Implementation Practices:** Implementing these fairness-aware algorithms involves embedding checks at multiple stages of the AI modeling process, from data collection to output analysis. Continuous monitoring for bias and feedback mechanisms are established to dynamically update the models to ensure they remain as objective as possible.

By deeply understanding these components of AI deployment in spatial data analysis, stakeholders can harness the full potential of AI technology, ensuring more accurate, efficient, and ethical use of spatial information in diverse applications. This expertise does not just empower data scientists but also broadens the horizons in planning and decision-making processes across urban development, environmental conservation, and more.

Artificial intelligence is significantly reshaping the landscape of spatial data management and processing. The enhancements we've discussed—ranging from sophisticated AI algorithms for effective data analysis to advanced computational solutions like cloud computing and specialized hardware—illustrate substantial progress in this field. These advancements streamline the analysis of vast and complex spatial datasets, which traditionally posed significant challenges in terms of both scale and accuracy.

Further, the integration of AI in spatial data handling has not only improved the efficiency and accuracy of data processing but has also brought forth new capabilities like real-time analysis and predictive analytics. These functionalities are invaluable, particularly for applications requiring timely decisions such as urban planning and environmental monitoring.

Looking ahead, the future of AI in spatial data promises even greater innovations. The next wave of advancements could include more intelligent and autonomous systems capable of learning from past data to predict future spatial scenarios with greater precision. Moreover, as AI continues to evolve, we can anticipate a more seamless integration with IoT and other technologies, leading to smarter cities and more responsive environmental management systems.

These innovations will continually enhance our ability to understand and interact with the physical spaces around us, making AI an indispensable tool in spatial data management and processing. As we move forward, the potential for AI to further transform this field remains vast and profoundly promising.

SPATIAL PROBLEM SOLVING IN AI

Investigating sophisticated spatial problem-solving techniques employed by AI across different sectors such as healthcare, urban planning, and logistics.

Spatial problem solving in AI represents a critical evolution in how machines understand and interact with the physical world around us. By integrating spatial awareness with artificial intelligence, industries such as healthcare and urban planning are witnessing revolutionary changes in operational efficiency and decision-making accuracy. AI's ability to analyze spatial data—ranging from mapping patient disease patterns to optimizing urban infrastructure—serves as a cornerstone for innovations that significantly enhance service delivery and management.

In healthcare, spatial AI transforms how medical data are utilized, enabling precise diagnostics and tailored treatment plans that account for individual variability. This capability not only speeds up patient care but also enhances the accuracy of diagnoses, potentially saving lives by catching anomalies that human eyes might miss. Similarly, in urban planning, AI uses spatial data to create smarter cities. It intelligently addresses traffic flow, resource distribution, and development strategies, ensuring sustainable and functional urban spaces that adapt to the needs of their populations.

These applications of spatial AI demonstrate its immense potential to solve complex, real-world problems by providing a lens through which vast amounts of data can be interpreted swiftly and accurately. As we continue to explore this fascinating intersection of geography and machine learning, the implications for future advancements promise even greater integration of AI in daily processes across various sectors, making our systems more intelligent and responsive to our spatial needs.

Spatial intelligence in AI refers to the capacity of artificial systems to manage and interpret data that has geographical or spatial information. This encompasses everything from recognizing the arrangement of objects in space to navigating and planning routes in dynamic environments. The ability to process this kind of data effectively is crucial for applications ranging from autonomous driving to environmental monitoring.

At its core, spatial intelligence in AI is built on several key components:

1. **Data Acquisition**: This involves collecting spatial data using various methods such as sensors, satellites, or cameras. For instance, drones capturing topographic images provide detailed insights into land use patterns.

2. **Data Processing and Analysis**: Once collected, the data must be processed. This includes tasks such as cleaning data, detecting patterns, and interpreting these patterns using machine learning algorithms. Advanced image recognition technologies, for example, can analyze satellite images to monitor changes in forest cover or urban development over time.

3. **Decision Making**: AI uses the analyzed data to make decisions or to provide recommendations. In autonomous vehicles, this involves real-time processing of spatial data to

navigate roads and avoid obstacles.

The critical role of spatial intelligence in AI becomes evident when interpreting complex environmental data. For example, AI systems equipped with spatial intelligence can predict flood patterns by analyzing changes in landscape and water flow data. This capability not only enhances our understanding of environmental phenomena but also aids in disaster management and planning.

Spatial intelligence in AI, however, is not without its challenges. Data quality, for instance, can significantly affect the insights derived from spatial analysis. Furthermore, the ethical implications concerning data privacy, especially data that can be traced back to specific locations or individuals, require careful consideration.

Understanding spatial intelligence in AI offers profound benefits and shows how our interaction with the vast amounts of data generated from our surroundings can be transformed into actionable knowledge. As technology advances, the integration of sophisticated spatial analysis tools in AI systems is set to expand, promising more innovative solutions across various sectors.

Let's take a deeper look at the machine learning algorithms pivotal to the data processing and analysis phase in spatial intelligence within AI, and also explore how data privacy is maintained.

Machine Learning Algorithms in Spatial AI:

- **Supervised Learning:**
- **Decision Trees:** These are used to make sequential decisions on spatial data attributes to classify or predict outcomes, such as identifying different types of land cover from satellite images based on features like color, texture, and moisture levels.
- **Support Vector Machines (SVM):** SVMs are effective in classifying complex spatial patterns. For example, they can differentiate urban from rural areas in aerial imagery by defining hyperplanes that distinctly categorize different regions based on input features such as building density and green space.
- **Neural Networks:** Neural networks, particularly convolutional neural networks (CNNs), excel in image classification tasks. They automatically detect important spatial features from large sets of training data, which makes them ideal for classifying land use or detecting changes in vegetation over time.

- **Unsupervised Learning:**
- **K-Means Clustering:** This algorithm groups data points with similar characteristics into clusters. In spatial data analysis, it helps in segmenting images based on similarities in pixel values, useful in distinguishing different natural formations in satellite photos.
- **Principal Component Analysis (PCA):** PCA reduces the dimensionality of spatial data by transforming a large set of variables into a smaller set that still contains most of the information in large datasets. This is particularly useful in noise reduction and feature extraction from satellite imagery data.

- <u>Reinforcement Learning:</u>
- In spatial AI, reinforcement learning algorithms optimize decision-making processes by learning behaviors through trial and error. This method is used in autonomous vehicle routing, where the AI system continuously learns the best routes and maneuvers based on real-time road conditions and obstacles.

<u>Data Privacy Measures in Spatial AI:</u>
- **<u>Data Anonymization:</u>** Removing any identifiable markers from spatial datasets before analysis to ensure individual or location privacy cannot be compromised.
- **<u>Differential Privacy:</u>** Implementing methods that add randomness to the data being processed, allowing for patterns and useful information to be analyzed without exposing individual data points.
- **<u>Secure Multi-party Computation:</u>** This technique enables multiple parties to jointly analyze data while ensuring that each party's data inputs remain private. It's crucial in scenarios where spatial data from various sources are pooled for urban planning or environmental monitoring.

Understanding these algorithms and privacy measures not only enhances comprehension of how spatial data is processed but also underlines the responsibilities involved in handling such data ethically. This clarity in the intricate components of spatial intelligence highlights both technological capabilities and the ongoing commitment to maintaining privacy and ethical standards in AI applications.

Imagine spatial AI in healthcare as akin to a highly skilled surgeon, equipped not with a scalpel but with vast data and precise algorithms. Just as a surgeon uses their expertise to identify and diagnose the nuances of human health with precision, spatial AI interprets intricate medical data to pinpoint health issues with remarkable accuracy.

Like a surgeon carefully navigating key points of an operation, spatial AI examines layers of medical imagery, from X-rays to MRI scans, to detect abnormalities such as tumors or fractures. Its precision is like that of a seasoned surgeon who can discern between tissues at a glance, enabling it to identify health problems early and accurately. This capability not only assists doctors in making informed decisions but also enhances patient outcomes by targeting the exact nature of the ailment without unnecessary interventions.

Moreover, just as a surgeon adapts to the complexities of each unique surgical case, spatial AI tailors its analysis to the individual patient, considering vast amounts of historical and real-time data to offer personalized diagnostic insights. This adaptation ensures that each patient receives care that is specifically configured to their health scenario, much like how a surgeon's approach varies from one operation to another based on the patient's specific conditions.

Thus, the role of spatial AI in healthcare is transformative, offering a level of precision and personalization that parallels the meticulous work of surgeons. This not only revolutionizes how diagnoses are performed but also profoundly impacts the broader healthcare landscape, leading to more efficient, effective, and personalized patient care.

Here is the detailed breakdown on the specific processes and technologies used by spatial AI in healthcare for diagnosing diseases:

- **Image Processing Techniques:**
  - **Segmentation:**
  - AI uses segmentation algorithms to divide medical imaging into regions representing different tissues or organs. This allows AI systems to isolate areas of interest, such as tumors or lesions, from normal anatomical structures to analyze each section for abnormalities, enhancing diagnosis precision.
  - **Feature Extraction:**
  - Feature extraction algorithms analyze segmented images to quantify characteristics such as the shape, size, or texture of a detected abnormality. This may include measuring the dimensions of a tumor or assessing the density of bone tissue, providing critical data that can influence diagnosis and treatment plans.

- **Machine Learning Algorithms Employed:**
  - **Convolutional Neural Networks (CNNs):**
  - CNNs are adept in processing visual imagery and are extensively used in analyzing medical images. These networks work by extracting hierarchical features from raw images—starting from simple edges to more complex features like textures—making them exceptionally effective in recognizing patterns indicative of specific diseases.
  - **Support Vector Machines (SVMs):**
  - SVMs are utilized for their robust classification

capabilities, particularly in binary classification problems. In healthcare, SVMs can distinguish between normal and pathological images, for example, SVMs can categorize an X-ray image as displaying either malignant or benign features, based on the learning from training datasets.

- ### Real-Time Data Handling:
  - ### Data Stream Processing:
    - AI systems equipped with real-time data processing capabilities can analyze data from medical devices as it is generated. For instance, data streaming from MRI machines is processed on-the-fly to detect sudden changes in a patient's physiological state that may require immediate medical attention.
  - ### Dynamic Learning Models:
    - These models continuously learn from new data, adjusting their parameters to reflect the most current information. This adaptability is particularly crucial in healthcare, where a patient's condition may evolve rapidly, requiring AI systems to update their diagnoses or predictions based on the latest data inputs.

This breakdown not only offers a glimpse into the sophisticated world of spatial AI in healthcare but also underscores its impact on enhancing medical diagnostics. By leveraging these advanced algorithms and procedures, spatial AI transforms vast amounts of medical data into actionable, precise, and personalized insights, fundamentally changing the landscape of healthcare delivery and patient management.

Imagine artificial intelligence (AI) as a city planner with an extraordinary vision. Just as a city planner reviews demographics, inspects road networks, and forecasts future urban growth, spatial intelligence equips AI with the ability to analyze vast amounts of data on population dynamics, traffic patterns, and infrastructural needs. This allows it to design smarter urban environments that are not only efficient but also adaptable to future challenges.

Think of how a planner uses maps and models to understand where to allocate resources or to plan new road constructions. Similarly, AI with spatial intelligence can process satellite images and traffic data to identify the busiest routes and predict where congestion might occur. With this knowledge, it can suggest optimal alterations to traffic lights or propose where a new road should be built to alleviate traffic pressure.

Moreover, as populations grow and cities expand, a good planner must forecast and adapt to these changes. AI uses predictive analytics, a fundamental part of spatial intelligence, to envision how cities will evolve based on current trends. This helps in planning essential services such as schools and hospitals to cater to increased demand effectively.

Thus, AI as a city planner doesn't just work with the present data but also anticipates the future needs of the urban landscape. This capability ensures cities are not just manageable today but remain vibrant and functional for future generations, illustrating the profound impact of spatial intelligence in urban development. This holistic approach speaks to both the complexity and the necessity of integrating advanced AI in our urban planning processes, making our cities smarter and more responsive to our evolving needs.

Here is the breakdown on the specific technologies and methodologies AI uses in urban planning:

- ## Data Collection Techniques:
  - ### Satellite Imagery:
    - AI harnesses the power of satellite imagery to monitor and analyze changes in urban environments over time. This includes assessing the expansion of urban areas, the state of infrastructure, and land use classifications. Advanced algorithms process these images to detect patterns of growth, areas of heavy construction, and changes in green spaces within cities.
  - ### Sensors:
    - Internet of Things (IoT) sensors play a crucial role in urban planning by providing real-time data on various aspects of the urban environment. This includes traffic flow, parking availability, air quality, and energy usage. AI systems analyze this data to identify trends, predict potential issues, and suggest improvements in real-time, such as optimizing traffic signals to reduce congestion during rush hours.

- ## Analysis Techniques:
  - ### Predictive Analytics:
    - AI employs predictive analytics to forecast future urban growth and infrastructure requirements. This is done using historical data trends and machine learning models that analyze factors like population growth, economic indicators,

and housing demand. These insights help urban planners in making informed decisions about where and how to develop future projects sustainably.

- Real-time Processing:

- Real-time data processing is vital for dynamic urban management. AI systems are equipped to process information as it comes in, allowing city administrators to react immediately to various situations. Examples include adjusting public transport routes on-the-fly in response to events or emergencies, or managing utilities more efficiently based on current demand.

- Decision-Making Algorithms:
- Machine Learning Models:

- Machine learning models in AI are trained on vast datasets to recognize complex patterns and predict outcomes in urban development. These models analyze data from past urban planning initiatives to determine the most effective strategies for sustainable development, such as where to place new parks or how to design road networks to minimize traffic.

- Simulation Models:

- AI uses advanced simulation models to visualize and predict the results of urban planning decisions before they are implemented. This might include simulating the impact of a new public transport system on traffic flow or how a new commercial district could affect local economies. These simulations help planners make decisions that are informed by a comprehensive analysis of potential outcomes.

This granular view into the use of AI in urban planning not only illustrates how data is utilized to enhance city living conditions but also emphasizes the adaptability of AI systems to meet future challenges, ensuring urban areas are not just livable but are poised for sustainable growth and development.

The integration of spatial AI in various sectors raises significant ethical considerations, primarily centered around privacy and fairness. The ability of spatial AI to analyze detailed geographical data can sometimes lead to the inadvertent exposure of personal information, making data privacy a paramount concern. Moreover, the potential for biased outputs due to skewed training datasets can result in unfair outcomes, affecting particular groups disproportionately.

To address these ethical challenges, several strategies are being implemented. Firstly, data anonymization techniques are extensively used to ensure that the information processed by spatial AI systems cannot be traced back to any individual. This involves altering the dataset so personal identifiers are removed, thus protecting individual privacy while allowing the valuable aspects of data to be utilized for analysis. For instance, in urban planning, while the AI might use location data to optimize traffic flow, the specifics of individual commuter routes are generalized to ensure privacy.

Secondly, fairness in AI outputs is being tackled through more equitable data collection methods and algorithmic audits. Diverse and representative data are crucial in training AI systems, as they prevent the perpetuation of biases that could occur if the training data is skewed towards a particular demographic. Algorithmic audits are systematic reviews conducted by independent parties that scrutinize AI systems for biased decision-making processes. By identifying and correcting biases, these audits help ensure that AI-based decisions are fair and equitable across all user groups.

Moreover, there is a growing emphasis on the development of ethical guidelines and standards for spatial AI applications, supported by international cooperation between tech companies, governments, and ethical watchdogs. These guidelines are aimed at harmonizing the approaches to AI ethics globally, providing a framework that helps developers and users of spatial AI navigate the complex moral landscape that comes with advanced technological capabilities.

By consciously addressing these ethical concerns, the deployment of spatial AI can be managed in a manner that not only enhances its benefits but also minimizes potential harms, promoting a more ethically-conscious application of this powerful technology. These efforts reflect a broader commitment to ensuring that advancements in AI contribute positively to society, bolstering trust in how new technologies are shaping the future.

Let's take a deeper look at the specific data anonymization techniques and algorithmic audits employed in spatial AI to ensure ethical standards are maintained:

- **Data Anonymization Techniques:**
  - **Technique Specifics:**

- **K-Anonymity:** This method ensures that individual data cannot be distinguished from at least k-1 other individuals who also appear in the dataset. It often involves generalization and suppression of identifiers to prevent linkage to real identities.

- **Differential Privacy:** This technique adds noise to the data or queries to the data in a way that the outcome of an analysis is the same, whether any individual data is included or not, thereby securing individual privacy while providing accurate outputs.

- **Pseudonymization:** Unlike complete anonymization, pseudonymization replaces private identifiers with fake identifiers or pseudonyms. While the data can still be attributed to a specific individual by using additional information, pseudonymization reduces the risk associated with data breaches.

- **Implementation Examples:**

- In urban planning, k-anonymity has been applied to mobile location data used to analyze traffic patterns without revealing specific user locations. Cities analyzing foot traffic through Wi-Fi signal mapping often employ differential privacy to ensure that individual paths through a city cannot be traced back to an identifiable person.

- **Algorithmic Audits:**
- **Audit Process:**
- **Initial Review:** Auditors examine the design and development of the AI system, focusing on the data inputs, algorithmic models, and the decision-making processes.

- **Testing Phase:** This involves running the algorithm through various scenarios to see how it behaves in different situations, particularly looking for outputs that indicate bias or unfair treatment.

- **Reporting:** Findings are documented with recommendations for improvement. This report is crucial for organizations to understand potential flaws in their AI systems.
- **Bias Detection and Correction:**
- Techniques such as statistical analysis involve examining data sets and output decisions for patterns that suggest bias. Comparative studies might be conducted between different demographic groups to ensure equitable treatment.
- Once identified, biases can be corrected by adjusting algorithm parameters or rebalancing the training datasets to represent a more diverse population.
- **Regulatory and Ethical Standards:**
- Specific standards like GDPR in the European Union dictate strict guidelines on algorithmic transparency and data privacy. Auditors often refer to such frameworks to ensure compliance and guide the process of ethical certification.

These detailed insights into the anonymization techniques and audit processes highlight the rigorous steps taken to ensure spatial AI operates within ethical bounds, safeguarding individual privacy and promoting fairness. This not only protects users but also enhances the credibility and acceptance of AI technologies in society.

Spatial problem solving in AI is poised for significant advancements that could further transform how we interact with our environment. Currently, AI excels at analyzing vast amounts of spatial data to optimize routes, manage city planning, and even assist in conservation efforts. The future, however, holds promise for even more intricate integrations of AI in spatial contexts that could make these systems more intuitive and effective.

One promising direction is the enhancement of AI's predictive capabilities. Future AI systems could move beyond reacting to real-time data and start anticipating changes well ahead of time, based on patterns observed over extended periods. This could be particularly crucial in areas like disaster management, where predicting events such as floods or forest fires before they occur can save lives and resources.

Additionally, the integration of more sophisticated machine learning models that can learn from less structured data could enable AI to handle more complex spatial problems such as navigating the chaotic environments of urban centers in developing countries, where formal mapping is less prevalent. These enhanced models could capture nuances that previous systems may have overlooked, improving user interaction and system reliability.

Augmented Reality (AR) and Virtual Reality (VR) could also play larger roles, making spatial problem-solving more interactive and user-friendly. Imagine urban planners or architects walking through a virtual representation of their projects, interacting with AI suggestions in real-time, and making modifications that instantly show potential outcomes.

Moreover, as AI technologies gain the ability to process spatial data with greater depth and nuance, ethical considerations must also evolve. Ensuring these systems are not only powerful but also equitable and transparent will be crucial. Enhanced ethical AI frameworks will ensure these innovations benefit all sectors of society without infringing on privacy or creating bias.

As AI in spatial problem solving continues to evolve, it will not only expand the borders of our technological capabilities but also redefine the landscape of our daily lives, making our interactions with space more efficient, safe, and sustainable.

REAL WORLD EXAMPLES OF SPATIAL AI

Spatial artificial intelligence (AI) is redefining the fabric of how decisions are made across various sectors, from urban planning and agriculture to disaster response and environmental conservation. This technology harnesses geographic data and machine learning to interpret and interact with the physical world in an unprecedented manner. Its capability to process and analyze spatial information not only enhances efficiency but also fosters innovation, paving the way for a deeper understanding of the complex interplay between various elements in our surroundings.

As we delve into real-world examples, the versatility of spatial AI unfolds through a series of transformative applications that demonstrate its potential impact. In cities, it orchestrates the flow of traffic and crowds; in fields, it guides tractors to sow and harvest with pinpoint accuracy; in forests, it tracks the patterns of wildlife; and in crisis zones, it strategizes rescues and resource distributions. Each instance provides a unique insight into how spatial AI is being tailored to meet specific challenges, offering solutions that are as varied as they are dynamic.

This exploration not only highlights the broad utility of spatial AI but also invites us to consider its future trajectory. As the technology evolves and becomes more integrated into our daily lives, understanding its current applications is crucial for envisioning the innovative ways it could further enhance societal functions tomorrow. Engage with these stories of contemporary AI application, and grasp a clearer view of the horizon where technology meets real-world challenges, transforming potentials into actualities.

During Michael Bloomberg's tenure as mayor, New York City pioneered the integration of spatial AI into its urban planning framework, particularly transforming its traffic systems and public transportation networks. This move was part of a broader initiative to make the city smarter and more responsive to the needs of its inhabitants.

The cornerstone of this integration was the implementation of an advanced traffic management system driven by spatial AI. This system utilized a vast array of sensors and cameras distributed throughout the city to collect real-time data on traffic conditions. Spatial AI algorithms analyzed this data to understand traffic patterns and predict bottlenecks before they occurred. For instance, if a traffic jam began to form on one avenue, the system could adjust traffic lights in real-time to redirect flow and alleviate congestion. This dynamic approach to traffic management not only reduced average travel times but also helped in cutting down emissions from idling vehicles.

Public transportation saw similar enhancements. Spatial AI was employed to optimize bus routes and schedules based on a myriad of factors, including passenger demand patterns, which were continually updated through real-time data. This not only improved the efficiency of the existing bus network but also enhanced rider experiences by reducing wait times and overcrowding.

These initiatives showcased the potential of spatial AI to make urban living more efficient. However, the integration was not without challenges. One significant issue was the privacy concerns raised over the extensive data collection required for these systems to function. The city administration had to navigate these concerns carefully, ensuring that data privacy regulations were strictly followed to maintain public trust.

This detailed focus on enhancing urban infrastructure through spatial AI under Bloomberg's administration not only modernized New York City's approach to municipal management but also served as a model for other cities worldwide, illustrating the actionable benefits of technology in urban planning. The success here emphasizes the potential and necessity of adopting such technologies in the face of growing urban challenges.

Let's take a deeper look at the sophisticated spatial AI algorithms and meticulous data privacy measures implemented for traffic management during Michael Bloomberg's administration in New York City.

- Spatial AI Algorithms for Traffic Management:
- Data Analysis Algorithms:
- The core of NYC's traffic management relied on predictive analytics and machine learning models. Using clustering algorithms, the system categorized segments of traffic data into normal and abnormal traffic patterns.

Decision trees and neural networks then analyzed these patterns, detecting anomalies that could lead to bottlenecks or traffic jams.

- For bottleneck prediction, the system employed regression models that considered historical data and real-time inputs such as vehicle speed, traffic density, and time of day to forecast traffic flow and potential disruptions.

- **Real-Time Decision-Making Algorithms:**

- Real-time adjustments to traffic control systems were powered by dynamic algorithms capable of rapid data processing. Rule-based algorithms evaluated current traffic conditions against pre-set thresholds to decide instant changes like traffic light durations.

- Optimization algorithms, such as linear programming, were applied to allocate resources efficiently, ensuring that adjustments like rerouting traffic or altering bus frequencies were implemented swiftly to mitigate any identified traffic issues effectively.

- **Data Privacy Measures:**
- **Techniques Used to Protect Data:**

- To protect the privacy of individuals whose data was captured by city sensors, differential privacy techniques were employed. This involved adding 'noise' to the data sets, ensuring that the data could be used for analysis without revealing the precise movements of individual vehicles or persons.

- Encryption methods and secure multi-party computation protocols were also used to safeguard data at rest and during transmission, thus enhancing the security of the information gathered from public spaces.

- **Compliance and Regulation Adherence:**

- The city administration rigorously adhered to privacy

laws such as the General Data Protection Regulation (GDPR) and local privacy standards. Regular audits were conducted to ensure compliance with these regulations.

- Collaborations with regulatory bodies and privacy experts helped to shape policies that governed the use of spatial AI in public administration, ensuring that all technological deployments were both legally compliant and ethically sound.

These elements collectively highlight the intricate balance New York City maintained between leveraging cutting-edge spatial AI technologies for enhanced urban management and ensuring robust privacy protections were in place. This dual focus not only optimized city traffic flows but also safeguarded the trust and rights of its residents, setting a benchmark for other global cities.

Imagine spatial AI in wildlife conservation as the ultimate, high-tech ranger in the vast wilderness. Much like Jane Goodall, who meticulously observed and recorded chimpanzee behaviors, spatial AI systems are tasked with monitoring wildlife patterns and habitat use, but with a digital precision that covers extensive geographical areas which human researchers cannot easily or quickly access.

These AI systems operate like a sophisticated network of trail cameras, but instead of taking occasional snapshots, they continuously gather and analyze myriad data points. Through satellite imagery and ground-based sensors, spatial AI tracks animal movements, vegetation changes, and even potential threats from illegal poaching or human encroachment. This ongoing surveillance can be likened to a

GPS system, not for navigation, but for understanding the intricate web of life within a conservation area.

In practice, employing spatial AI in projects like those led by Jane Goodall allows conservationists to observe patterns over time, such as migration routes or changes in animal behaviors, with the data providing insights that are vital for developing strategies to protect these species. For instance, if spatial AI detects unusual movement patterns in a wildlife reserve, this could signal disturbances that require immediate attention, whether it's encroaching human activity or environmental threats.

This integration of technology into conservation efforts transforms not just how data is collected, but how quickly and effectively it can be acted upon, making the preservation of biodiversity not only more manageable but more proactive. It embodies a powerful blend of technology and nature stewardship, illustrating a modern approach to conservation that is both strategic and sympathetic.

Here is the breakdown on the specific technologies and methodologies employed by spatial AI systems in wildlife conservation, laid out to provide clarity and understanding of each functional component:

- **<u>Types of Sensors Used in Spatial AI:</u>**
  - **<u>Satellite Sensors:</u>**
    - Capabilities: These high-altitude devices provide a macroscopic view of vast natural areas, enabling the monitoring of landscape changes over time, such as

deforestation or natural disaster impacts. They also track weather patterns, providing data crucial for anticipating environmental shifts that could affect wildlife.

- **Ground-based Sensors:**
  - Function: Positioned directly in the wildlife habitats, these sensors collect granular data on local environmental conditions like temperature, humidity, and even soil composition.
  - Animal Tracking: They are crucial for gathering precise movements of animal groups, which helps in studying migration routes and social behaviors.
  - Bioacoustic Monitoring: These sensors detect and analyze sounds made by wildlife, aiding in the monitoring of species that might be difficult to observe visually.

- **Data Processing Algorithms:**
  - **Image Recognition Algorithms:**
    - Usage: Employed to process the continuous stream of visual data captured by trail cameras and drones, these algorithms utilize techniques such as convolutional neural networks to automatically identify and classify wildlife species and their behaviors.
    - Conservation Application: Help in population counting and monitoring the health conditions of animals without human intrusion.
  - **Pattern Detection Algorithms:**
    - Detection Methods: These include statistical analysis and machine learning models designed to flag anomalous patterns in animal movements or environmental conditions that might suggest threats like poaching or unusual climatic conditions.
    - Threat Identification: Enable rapid response initiatives by highlighting areas of concern that require

immediate conservation action.

- **Real-time Response Mechanisms:**
  - **Automated Alerts:**
    - Mechanism: When the system detects unauthorized human activity or natural threats like wildfires close to protected areas, it triggers automatic alerts. These are relayed instantly to conservation managers and local enforcement units.
    - Implementation: Utilizes both the data from pattern detection algorithms and threshold settings predefined by conservation criteria.
  - **Dynamic Data Integration:**
    - Continuous Monitoring: Integrates data from multiple sensor types in real time, ensuring a comprehensive understanding of the current state of the conservation area.
    - Strategy Adaptation: Facilitates the dynamic adjustment of conservation strategies, like re-routing of patrol units based on the latest data insights, ensuring responses are both timely and relevant.

This detailed look not only illustrates how each component of spatial AI systems operates independently but also demonstrates their collective contribution towards the overarching goal of effective wildlife management and protection. By harnessing these sophisticated technologies, conservation efforts can be more targeted, proactive, and efficient, ultimately fostering a better symbiosis between humanity and nature.

Since the times of Norman Borlaug, the father of the Green Revolution, agriculture has undergone significant transformation, especially with the introduction and evolution of spatial AI. Borlaug's work in the mid-20th century catapulted agricultural productivity by developing high-yield crop varieties and improving farming practices. However, modern spatial AI technologies have expanded on these foundations by introducing precision agriculture, enabling farmers to maximize yields while minimizing resource use and environmental impact.

Spatial AI in agriculture today utilizes a variety of sophisticated techniques. One fundamental component involves the use of satellite imagery and drones equipped with sensors. These tools gather detailed data about field conditions, including soil moisture levels, temperature, and crop health. This data is then processed using advanced algorithms to detect patterns and anomalies, guiding decisions such as the optimal times for planting, watering, or applying fertilizers.

For instance, spatial AI can analyze the nitrogen content in the soil from aerial images to recommend precise fertilizer applications, ensuring that each part of a field receives a tailor-made treatment. This not only helps in conserving the amount of fertilizer used but also prevents runoff into nearby ecosystems, thus supporting sustainable farming practices.

However, the integration of spatial AI into farming is not without challenges. The technology requires significant investment in terms of both money and time, and there is a steep learning curve associated with using advanced AI tools effectively. Moreover, the reliance on high-quality, real-time data means that connectivity issues can disrupt the functioning of AI systems, potentially leading to missed farming opportunities or resource wastage.

Despite these challenges, the potential benefits of spatial AI in agriculture point towards a future where farming is more science-driven and responsive to the nuances of nature. This shift not only promises to uphold Borlaug's legacy of enhancing food security but also aligns with modern principles of environmental sustainability and economic efficiency, making it a critical area of investment for the future of global agriculture. Such progress not only represents an evolution of Borlaug's initial innovations but also a leap towards an era of farming that is both smart and considerate of planetary boundaries.

In the realm of modern agriculture, the integration of spatial AI through drones and satellites has revolutionized farming practices by providing critical data for decision making. This detailed guide outlines the step-by-step workflow of how spatial AI systems operate from data collection to actionable agricultural insights.

1. Data Collection:

Drones and satellites, equipped with advanced sensors, are primary tools for collecting agricultural data. These sensors include multi-spectral cameras that capture images beyond the visible range, providing detailed insights into crop health by detecting light reflection from plants. Soil sensors measure moisture levels and nutrient content, vital for assessing field conditions. Thermal cameras record heat signatures to help identify irrigation issues or disease outbreaks.

2. Data Processing:

The collected data undergoes rigorous analysis using sophisticated algorithms. Image recognition algorithms play a critical role here, particularly in analyzing crop health from aerial imagery. These algorithms can discern subtle differences in plant coloration and condition, indicative of health or distress. Machine learning models, such as regression analysis or neural networks, process soil data to predict moisture and nutrient levels, enabling precise predictions about crop needs.

3. Anomaly Detection:

Spatial AI utilizes statistical and machine learning techniques to detect anomalies that might indicate potential threats like pest infestations or diseases. Pattern recognition algorithms analyze historical and real-time data to identify deviation from normal growth patterns or environmental conditions. Clustering techniques can group similar anomalies together to help pinpoint specific issues across large farming areas.

4. Decision Support:

The processed data is then converted into actionable advice by AI systems. Algorithms generate recommendations for the optimal planting times, effective irrigation schedules, and precise amounts of fertilizer needed for specific areas of a crop field. This advice is typically disseminated through user-friendly interfaces on farm management software, assisting farmers in making informed decisions that align with sustainable farming practices.

5. Implementation and Feedback Loop:

Farmers implement these AI-driven recommendations in their fields. The effectiveness of these actions provides feedback to the AI systems, often collected through the same sensors or additional in-field assessments. This feedback is crucial for refining AI models. Continuous learning algorithms adjust their parameters based on outcome data, enhancing the accuracy and relevance of future recommendations.

This progression from data acquisition through drones and satellites to precise action recommendations encapsulates how spatial AI empowers farmers to maximize yield with minimal resource waste. The synergy between sophisticated technology and traditional farming creates a more efficient, sustainable agricultural environment, paving the way for a future where farming is driven by data, precision, and sustainability.

Imagine spatial AI in disaster response as the ultimate command center, similar to how a seasoned conductor leads a symphony, orchestrating each section to create a harmonious performance under pressure. In much the same way, spatial AI takes the lead during emergencies, coordinating efforts efficiently and effectively across a broad spectrum of resources and personnel. A vivid example of this can be seen in Elon Musk's initiatives, where technology meets pragmatism in times of crisis.

For instance, when hurricanes disrupted life and infrastructure, Musk's companies deployed spatial AI technologies to optimize resource allocation and route planning for recovery efforts. Think of it as having a high-tech overview, akin to playing a strategy video game where each move is calculated and every resource is optimized for maximum benefit. The AI systems analyze real-time data from satellites and drones, monitoring weather patterns and assessing damage to direct aid where it's needed most urgently.

In these scenarios, spatial AI functions much like a nerve center, receiving inputs from various sources—like a commander receiving reports from the field—and then swiftly making strategic decisions. It prioritizes tasks, deploys aid, and adjusts routes for emergency vehicles, avoiding blocked roads or dangerous conditions, ensuring help arrives as quickly as possible.

This approach not only exemplifies how cutting-edge technology can be harnessed to respond to natural disasters but also highlights the importance of such innovation in saving lives and rebuilding communities. Musk's use of spatial AI illustrates a future where technology's role in disaster response is not just supportive but pivotal, offering a beacon of hope and a blueprint for efficient crisis management. This is technology stepping out of labs and boardrooms, directly impacting the ground reality, proving that when we talk about innovation saving lives, it's not just a metaphor but a tangible truth.

Here is the breakdown on the specific technologies and operational strategies employed by spatial AI systems in disaster response, as exemplified by initiatives like those Elon Musk is involved in:

- **Data Collection Methods:**
  - **Satellite Imagery:**
    - Usage: Satellite imagery is crucial for assessing the overall impact of disasters across extensive areas. It helps in identifying the extent of damage, from flooded regions to razed forests, providing a macroscopic view that is vital for planning rescue and recovery efforts.
    - Integration: The imagery data is fed into spatial AI systems which process and analyze the area impacted, helping in the swift allocation of resources where they are needed most.
  - **Drone Surveillance:**
    - Function: Drones provide granular, real-time data on specific locations, crucial for areas that are hard to reach or where immediate human assessment is dangerous.
    - Connection with AI: Drones stream data directly to AI systems, which immediately analyze information such as building integrity, road blockages, and the presence of survivors, enabling timely updates and actions.

- **Data Processing Algorithms:**
  - **Pattern Recognition:**
    - Description: These algorithms analyze data from various sources to identify patterns indicating critical damage or potential further risks, like structural weaknesses in buildings or impending secondary disasters.
    - Application: Such algorithms prioritize areas requiring

urgent intervention, helping to streamline the response efforts effectively.

- Resource Optimization Algorithms:
- Function: Focus on allocating resources—including personnel, medical aid, and relief supplies—based on dynamic inputs such as severity of impact, urgency, and resource availability.
- Benefit: Ensures that resources are not just allocated but optimized to serve the most urgent needs first, enhancing the efficiency of responses.

- Decision-Making Framework:
- Automated Decision Systems:
- Setup: These systems make real-time decisions using AI, based on algorithms that process incoming data against a set of predetermined response protocols.
- Execution: They trigger actions like alerting response teams, activating emergency services, and mobilizing equipment without waiting for human intervention, speeding up the response time.

- Human-AI Collaboration:
- Integration: Real-time data from AI analyses is relayed to human operators who then make nuanced decisions that require human judgment.
- Synergy: This collaboration ensures that while AI provides speed and data processing capability, human expertise guides the strategic and ethical considerations of the response.

- Implementation Strategies:
- Rapid Deployment:
- Approach: Logistical AI systems analyze routes and

resource locations to propose the fastest pathways for delivering aid.

- Result: This capability significantly reduces the time it takes for aid to reach affected zones, which can be crucial for saving lives.

- **Feedback Loops:**

- Concept: Feedback from each deployment phase is used to adjust and improve AI models continuously.

- Adaptation: These loops ensure that the systems learn from every incident, enhancing future responses to be more aligned with practical, on-ground realities.

This comprehensive breakdown showcases how spatial AI acts as a dynamic and efficient command center during disasters, with each of its components playing a crucial role in ensuring that disaster response is as effective and immediate as possible. These systems represent a significant leap in how technology can be harnessed to safeguard and assist in human crises.

Spatial AI is rapidly reshaping industries, driven by advancements that promise to enhance both efficiency and accuracy across various domains. As this technology continues to evolve, it is poised to further revolutionize fields such as healthcare, agriculture, urban planning, and disaster management. The integration of more sophisticated machine learning models and increased data processing capabilities will enable spatial AI systems to predict outcomes with greater precision, manage resources more effectively, and ultimately deliver solutions that are both innovative and sustainable.

In healthcare, for example, spatial AI could transform how medical resources are allocated, ensuring that facilities in high-demand areas are adequately equipped. In agriculture, ongoing enhancements in AI-driven crop analysis will assist farmers in maximizing yields while minimizing environmental impacts. Urban planning will benefit from smarter, more livable city designs that optimize space and resources, catering efficiently to growing populations. Moreover, as witnessed in disaster response efforts, the ability to analyze data in real time and make prompt, informed decisions can significantly mitigate risks and enhance the effectiveness of relief operations.

The trajectory of spatial AI does not just suggest incremental changes but signifies a leap towards a future where decision-making is profoundly data-driven. The integration of IoT devices and smarter algorithms means that spatial AI will become more embedded in daily operations, turning the data collected into actionable insights that can preempt challenges and streamline processes. As industries adapt to these capabilities, the potential for transformative change is substantial, highlighting the pivotal role of spatial AI in crafting tomorrow's solutions from today's data. This progression underscores the critical importance of not just observing but actively participating in the evolution of spatial AI to harness its full potential responsibly and innovatively.

FUTURE TRENDS IN SPATIAL AI

Spatial AI is already revolutionizing how decisions are made in fields ranging from urban planning to environmental conservation. It navigates cars, orchestrates traffic flows, and even monitors wildlife across expansive natural reserves. As we stand on the brink of these current applications, the technology is not just a tool of the present but a promise to the future. Today, we are poised to discuss not simply what spatial AI is, but what it could become. The upcoming innovations hold potential not merely to follow trends but to set them, promising transformations that could redefine the interface between technology and daily life.

This chapter shifts focus to the horizon, to what lies ahead for spatial AI. It explores how emerging advancements might further integrate into our lives, becoming more predictive, responsive, and perhaps even anticipatory. From smarter cities that dynamically adapt to their inhabitants' needs to disaster response systems that can strategically mitigate risks before they escalate, spatial AI is set to go beyond current functionalities to more proactive realms.

As you delve into this discussion, you'll find a clear, coherent exploration of complex ideas broken down into straightforward, engaging explanations. This is where the future of spatial AI is not just outlined but brought into relatable clarity, demonstrating its profound potential to impact our world, lifestyles, and the broader environment.

Join in uncovering the layers of this evolving technology, where each page aims to not only inform but also inspire the imagination about the possibilities that lie in harnessing the power of spatial AI.

Upcoming enhancements in AI technology are poised to significantly advance the capabilities of spatial AI, particularly in its ability to make dynamic and real-time decisions. This progress hinges largely on improvements in data processing speeds and the sophistication of algorithms, which enable the system to interpret and respond to complex environmental data with unprecedented accuracy and efficiency.

Consider an example of urban traffic management, a realm where spatial AI is already making strides. Future improvements might allow the system to not only manage current traffic flows but also predict and mitigate potential bottlenecks before they occur. This is achieved through advanced algorithms that analyze real-time data from myriad sensors across a city to model traffic scenarios and adjust signals and routes instantaneously. Such capability translates to reduced congestion, shorter travel times, and lower emissions—outcomes that underscore the practical benefits of enhanced decision-making precision.

Furthermore, these advancements extend to more critical applications such as emergency response and disaster management. In situations like natural disasters, where every second counts, improved spatial AI can quickly analyze data from satellite imagery and ground sensors to ascertain the most impacted areas and efficiently coordinate rescue operations. This rapid data processing and decision-making capacity can significantly enhance the speed and efficacy of emergency responses, potentially saving lives.

Each of these scenarios reveals how improvements in AI technology not only refine the operational aspects of spatial AI but also broaden its impact across various sectors. By breaking down complex data sets into actionable intelligence swiftly, spatial AI is transforming into a more robust tool that can handle the dynamic demands of the real world. As these technologies mature, they promise to deliver solutions that are not only innovative but also integral to advancing human interaction with increasingly complex environments.

Attempt 1 failed with status code 520. Retrying...
Let's take a closer look at the intricate technologies and methodologies that drive the dynamic real-time decision-making capabilities of spatial AI, breaking down how each component works and contributes to overall system efficiency.

- **Data Processing Speed Enhancements:**
- **Hardware Innovations:** The realm of hardware has seen significant advancements that bolster the data processing capabilities of spatial AI systems. Modern GPUs (Graphics Processing Units) have been tailored to handle parallel operations, which split complex tasks into simpler subtasks that are processed simultaneously, dramatically speeding up data handling. Additionally, specialized AI chips, also known as AI accelerators, are designed specifically to perform AI tasks more efficiently than standard CPUs. These chips accelerate the execution of AI

algorithms, particularly those involving neural networks.

- **Optimization Techniques:** To further reduce latency, which is critical for applications like autonomous driving or real-time surveillance, data workflows are optimized through techniques such as parallel processing. This involves distributing data across multiple processors to speed up data handling. Another key technique is edge computing, which processes data near the data source rather than sending it to distant data centers. This minimizes delay and speeds up response times in critical applications.

- ## Algorithmic Sophistication in Spatial AI:
- **Real-Time Analysis Algorithms:** Spatial AI employs a range of machine learning models and heuristic approaches to analyze data in real-time. Machine learning models, like convolutional neural networks (CNNs), are adept at processing and making sense of visual data from environmental sensors, enabling systems to understand and interact with their surroundings swiftly. Heuristic algorithms provide a framework for decision-making that simulates human-like reasoning, helping to quickly evaluate multiple possible conditions and scenarios.

- **Predictive Algorithms for Traffic Management:** In managing traffic, spatial AI uses predictive algorithms to anticipate and mitigate potential bottlenecks and optimize traffic flow. These algorithms often utilize queuing theory to model traffic as flows and queues, predicting future congestion and enabling preemptive adjustments. Neural networks can predict traffic patterns based on historical data and real-time inputs, adjusting signals and routes dynamically to prevent congestion.

- **Decision-Making Algorithms in Emergency Management:** For rapid decision-making in emergency management, spatial AI relies on algorithms such as decision trees, which help in making sequential decisions quickly in evolving situations. Rule-based systems use a set of predefined rules to make decisions based on current data inputs. Meanwhile, reinforcement learning, a type of machine learning, enables the system to learn the best actions to take in real-time from direct interaction with the environment, improving response strategies dynamically.

By delving into these technologies, one gains a deeper understanding of how spatial AI functions at a fundamental and advanced level, turning vast data inputs into precise, actionable decisions almost instantaneously. This capability is not just revolutionary but essential, as it forms the backbone of numerous applications that require immediacy and accuracy, from urban planning to critical rescue operations. This detailed exploration helps illuminate the sophisticated underpinnings of spatial AI systems, highlighting their importance and vast potential in our increasingly interconnected and automated world.

Think of spatial AI in environmental sciences as a high-tech guardian, much like a well-equipped park ranger who is everywhere at once, keeping a vigilant eye on the vast expanses of our planet. This technology, equipped with a suite of tools from satellite imaging to ground sensors, stands watch, tirelessly monitoring ecological changes. Whether it's tracking deforestation, observing melting ice caps, or monitoring urban sprawl, spatial AI helps scientists to see the big picture and the minute details of environmental shifts with precision.

Imagine a world where spatial AI is the smoke detector for impending forest fires or the early warning system for coral bleaching. It detects subtle changes in vegetation, water levels, and land use that might elude the human eye. By analyzing data continuously collected from around the globe, spatial AI can alert us to critical shifts in real-time, thereby enabling timely interventions to mitigate the impacts of climate change and habitat loss.

Moreover, spatial AI doesn't just report problems; it also provides solutions. By crunching vast amounts of environmental data, it can help strategize reforestation projects, manage water resources wisely, and plan urban developments sustainably. It's like having a master strategist in environmental management, one that computes the most efficient ways to heal and protect our planet.

So, as we sip our coffee and ponder the world around us, it's comforting to know that spatial AI serves as both a shield and a strategist, offering not just surveillance but also solutions to some of the most pressing environmental challenges of our times. This integration of technology in environmental sciences isn't just innovative; it's essential, acting as a cornerstone for future conservation efforts, ensuring that we and generations to come inherit a healthier planet.

Here is the breakdown of the specific technologies and methods employed by spatial AI in monitoring and managing environmental changes, presented to enhance your understanding of how this advanced tool functions in the real world:

- **Types of Sensors Used in Spatial AI for Environmental Monitoring:**
  - **Satellite Sensors:**
  - Capabilities: These sensors provide a bird's-eye view, capturing large-scale environmental data from above. They are instrumental in tracking phenomena like deforestation, changes in ice caps, and even patterns of desertification.
  - Use Cases: By observing changes in vegetation and water bodies, satellite sensors help identify areas at risk, enabling preemptive measures against environmental degradation.
  - **Ground Sensors:**
  - Monitoring: Positioned directly in various environments, these sensors collect detailed, localized data. For example, they measure soil moisture in agricultural fields or detect air quality in urban areas.
  - Functionality: This localized data is crucial for understanding how environmental changes affect specific areas, aiding in targeted action such as watering crops efficiently or tackling urban air pollution.

- **Data Processing Techniques in Spatial AI:**
  - **Real-Time Analysis:**
  - Process: Data from both satellite and ground sensors is aggregated and analyzed swiftly to detect immediate environmental threats. This analysis happens in real time, providing up-to-the-minute accuracy.
  - Examples: Immediate detection of unexpected forest fires or sudden floods, enabling quicker response and potentially mitigating damage.
  - **Long-Term Trend Analysis:**
  - Mechanism: Using historical data sets, machine

learning models identify patterns and predict long-term environmental shifts. This analysis helps in making informed decisions about future challenges.

- Applications: Strategic planning like reforestation, where understanding past trends aids in deciding where and how to plant trees effectively to combat desertification.

- AI Models Used in Environmental Strategies:
- Predictive Models:

- Function: These models use varied data inputs to forecast possible future scenarios of environmental change. They evaluate multiple variables and their possible impacts, predicting outcomes like potential flooding or drought conditions.

- Strategic Use: Helps in planning interventions such as building flood defenses or creating drought-resistant crop planting strategies.

- Decision Support Systems:

- Role: These systems compile insights from predictive models and real-time analyses to support decision-making processes.

- Benefits: They provide actionable recommendations for resource management and urban planning, ensuring that decisions are data-driven and environmentally considerate.

Through this detailed exploration, it becomes clear how spatial AI serves as both a vigilant monitor and a strategic advisor in the domain of environmental science. By harnessing these technologies, we can not only react more adeptly to immediate threats but also plan more effectively for sustainable future developments.

Spatial AI is poised to redefine the realms of virtual (VR) and augmented reality (AR), enhancing how users interact with digital environments through deeper integration of real-world context and sophisticated data interpretation. This technology equips VR and AR systems with the ability to understand and manipulate physical space in complex ways, offering a more immersive and intuitive experience for users.

Breaking down this integration, consider the role of spatial AI in VR and AR as akin to giving these technologies a sense of 'sight' and 'awareness' of their surroundings. For instance, in an AR application, spatial AI allows the system to recognize and respond to the physical layout of a room, dynamically placing digital objects that interact logically with real-world constructs like tables or walls. These interactions are not statically programmed but are determined in real time, adapting as the user moves about the space. This capability is powered by advanced algorithms that process spatial data collected from cameras and sensors to accurately map environments and place virtual elements precisely within them.

In VR, the impact of spatial AI extends to creating more lifelike and responsive environments. It can simulate realistic scenarios by incorporating physical laws of motion and spatial constraints, enhancing the training modules for fields such as medical surgery or heavy machinery operation. These simulations require precise spatial computations to ensure that virtual tools interact believably with the virtual world, enhancing both the learning efficacy and user engagement.

Moreover, as spatial AI grows more sophisticated, it could lead to breakthroughs in multi-user interactions in both VR and AR by synchronizing spatial information among multiple users in different locations. This would enable a form of spatial coherence where users, irrespective of their real-world location, can interact with the same virtual objects or environments in a consistent and reliable manner, bringing a new level of collaboration to areas such as remote learning, virtual meetings, and social interactions.

While the prospects are promising, the implementation of spatial AI in VR and AR must navigate challenges such as ensuring privacy in data usage, maintaining low latency for real-time interactions, and overcoming hardware limitations. As these technologies evolve, harnessing the full potential of spatial AI will require not only technical innovations but also careful consideration of ethical and logistical concerns.

Understanding the role of spatial AI in transforming virtual and augmented realities provides a window into a future where digital and physical realms merge more seamlessly than ever before. It portrays a landscape where our interactions with digital content are as natural and intuitive as those in the real world, fundamentally changing how we learn, work, and connect.

Spatial AI integrates complex algorithms, advanced data processing techniques, and robust hardware configurations to enhance user experiences in virtual (VR) and augmented reality (AR) environments. This technical breakdown explores how these components work in concert to create immersive and responsive digital worlds.

Spatial Recognition Algorithms:

Spatial AI employs several machine learning models to interpret data from sensors and cameras effectively. Convolutional Neural Networks (CNNs) are widely used for their proficiency in handling image data, enabling the system to identify and understand spatial relationships within digital environments. This capability is crucial for AR applications where digital elements must interact seamlessly with the physical world. Another model, the Recurrent Neural Network (RNN), excels in dealing with sequences, making it ideal for tracking movements within VR spaces, where user paths or interactions need continuous assessment for a dynamic response.

Data Processing Techniques:

To manage and process the vast data streams generated by VR and AR applications, spatial AI leverages several sophisticated techniques. Parallel processing is employed to divide complex data tasks into smaller, manageable parts that are processed simultaneously, drastically reducing the time required for data handling. Edge computing plays a critical role by processing data closer to the source—such as on local servers or devices—which minimizes latency and enhances the real-time interaction essential for VR and AR experiences. Additionally, cloud-based solutions are utilized to scale data storage and computational power, accommodating the extensive data needs of immersive AR and VR applications without compromising performance.

Hardware Considerations:

The hardware ecosystem for implementing spatial AI in VR and AR is anchored by high-performance GPUs and specialized AI chips. GPUs excel in managing the intense graphical demands of VR and AR, providing the necessary power to render complex 3D environments smoothly. AI chips, specifically designed to handle machine learning operations efficiently, support the rapid interpretation of sensor and camera data crucial for spatial recognition tasks. Sensor technology, including LIDAR and infrared sensors, is also vital, offering precise environment mapping and user positioning, which are foundational for creating interactive, realistic VR and AR experiences.

Real-World Implementation Challenges:

Implementing spatial AI in VR and AR is not without challenges. Ethically, ensuring user data privacy is paramount, necessitating robust data encryption and anonymization techniques to prevent misuse. Logistically, reducing latency is critical to maintaining the immersive quality of VR and AR; techniques such as network slicing and 5G implementation are being explored to address this issue. From a hardware perspective, scalability poses another challenge; ongoing research focuses on developing more compact and energy-efficient AI chips that can deliver the required computational power without the constraints of current bulkier systems.

Understanding these technical aspects highlights the sophistication and potential of spatial AI in transforming VR and AR technologies. By addressing the practical challenges and leveraging the capabilities of advanced algorithms, data processing techniques, and hardware configurations, spatial AI is set to redefine how we interact with digital environments, making these experiences more intuitive, immersive, and accessible.

Spatial AI is dramatically reshaping industrial processes, ushering in a new era of efficiency and sustainability in sectors ranging from manufacturing to precision agriculture. At its core, spatial AI involves utilizing advanced location-based intelligence to optimize and automate complex industrial tasks, which are foundational to innovation in these fields.

Consider the manufacturing sector, where spatial AI implements real-time monitoring and control systems within factories. By integrating data from various sensors placed throughout a facility, AI models can predict machine failures before they occur, schedule maintenance proactively, and even streamline the production lines based on real-time demand data and supply chain conditions. This approach not only minimizes downtime but also boosts overall productivity by ensuring that operations run smoothly and continuously.

In the realm of precision agriculture, spatial AI transforms traditional farming techniques with its ability to analyze data from satellite images and field sensors. This technology enables farmers to monitor crop health at a granular level, determine the exact amount of water, fertilizers, and pesticides needed, and precisely time their applications. Such targeted interventions not only increase crop yields but also reduce resource waste, contributing significantly to sustainable agricultural practices.

These applications reveal spatial AI's pivotal role in driving not just incremental improvements but transformative changes across industries. The technology's ability to gather, process, and analyze vast amounts of spatial data in real-time helps industries not only to react to current conditions but also to anticipate future challenges and opportunities, fostering a proactive approach to innovation.

However, the integration of spatial AI also faces challenges, particularly in terms of data privacy, the complexity of implementation across varied environments, and the initial cost of setup. Addressing these issues requires a balanced approach of technological advancement with strategic policy frameworks and ongoing workforce training to fully harness the potential of spatial AI in industrial applications.

Overall, spatial AI stands as a cornerstone technology that promises to refine the efficiency and sustainability of industries. Its ongoing development and integration will likely continue to spur significant advancements, making industrial processes smarter and more adaptable to the changing global landscape. As we engage with this technology, we gain not only enhanced operational capabilities but also insights into a more sustainable and innovative future.

Let's take a deeper look at the sophisticated web of technologies that underpin spatial AI's implementation in manufacturing and precision agriculture. This exploration will provide insights into how these advanced systems work to enhance efficiency and sustainability across industries.

- **Algorithms Used in Spatial AI:**
  - **Predictive Maintenance Algorithms:** In the realm of manufacturing, machine learning models such as decision trees, support vector machines, and neural networks are employed to predict equipment failures. These models analyze data gathered from sensors to detect anomalies and patterns indicative of wear or impending breakdowns. This capability allows for preemptive maintenance scheduling, reducing unexpected downtime and extending machinery life.
  - **Optimization Algorithms for Supply Chain Management:** To manage the dynamic nature of supply chains, spatial AI utilizes complex optimization algorithms like genetic algorithms and linear programming. These algorithms assess real-time data concerning inventory levels, production rates, and logistics to dynamically adjust production schedules and distribution plans, ensuring efficiency and reducing wastage.

- **Types of Sensors Used:**
  - **In Manufacturing:** Industries often deploy a variety of sensors to maintain quality and operational stability. Vibration sensors monitor anomalies in equipment, suggesting potential failures. Optical sensors, on the other hand, are crucial for inspecting assembly lines to ensure that product quality meets the required standards.
  - **In Precision Agriculture:** Field sensors play a pivotal role. Soil moisture sensors help farmers understand the

hydration levels of crops at a granular level, leading to more precise irrigation, while multispectral sensors on drones or satellites assess plant health by capturing data across different wavelengths, detecting issues like pest infestations or nutrient deficiencies.

- **Data Processing Techniques:**
  - **Edge Computing in Spatial AI:** In manufacturing settings, edge computing devices process data directly at the source — machinery and sensors on the production floor. This setup minimizes latency, allowing for real-time analytics and immediate corrective actions, which is critical in maintaining uninterrupted production lines.
  - **Cloud-Based Data Analytics for Agriculture:** The integration and analysis of vast amounts of data collected from field sensors, satellites, and drones are often processed in the cloud. This centralized approach enables comprehensive analysis and generates actionable insights that assist in effective farm management strategies, from crop rotation planning to advanced resource allocation.

By breaking down these components, one gains a clearer understanding of how spatial AI not only supports but significantly propels industrial and agricultural sectors towards more innovative, efficient, and sustainable practices. This detailed examination helps illustrate the tangible impacts of spatial AI, contextualizing its importance in the modern industrial landscape. The fusion of these advanced algorithms, diverse sensor technologies, and adept data processing techniques illustrates a robust infrastructure that is transforming industry norms and practices.

The widespread adoption of spatial AI brings to light a number of ethical dilemmas and governance challenges that necessitate a thoughtful and rigorous approach to implementation. As spatial AI technologies become more embedded in our daily lives, the need for frameworks that ensure their responsible and equitable use becomes paramount. These frameworks should address key concerns such as privacy, data security, and the potential for bias, all while fostering transparency and accountability.

Privacy emerges as a primary concern, as spatial AI systems often rely on extensive data that can include sensitive personal information. Ensuring that this data is handled securely and that privacy is protected requires robust encryption methods and stringent data access controls. Furthermore, transparent policies must be established to inform users about what data is collected and how it is used, providing them with clear choices about their data.

Bias in spatial AI, particularly in applications like predictive policing or resource allocation, is another critical issue. To mitigate this, it is vital to employ diverse training datasets and to continuously monitor and audit AI systems for fairness and accuracy. Addressing bias not only improves the technology's effectiveness but also enhances public trust in how these tools are applied.

Moreover, the governance of spatial AI must involve multidisciplinary teams including ethicists, technologists, and community stakeholders, ensuring that diverse perspectives shape the development and deployment of these technologies. Such an approach encourages the creation of standards and best practices that prioritize human rights and social values.

Instituting these frameworks isn't just about preventing misuse; it's about steering the development of spatial AI towards outcomes that are beneficial and just, reinforcing its potential as a tool for positive change in society. Effective governance will therefore not only address the immediate ethical and operational challenges but also lay the groundwork for sustainable innovation, making sure that spatial AI serves the public good while respecting individual rights and freedoms.

CONCLUSION

As we draw the curtains on our exploration within "AI Spatial Intelligence Explained," we reflect on a journey through a transformative landscape where the realms of artificial intelligence and spatial reasoning converge. This book has traversed through intricate dialogues between theoretical foundations and practical applications, revealing how spatial intelligence is not just an academic interest but a pivotal force driving technological advancements in AI.

We began by delving into the basics of spatial intelligence, understanding its role in human cognition, and extending these concepts to how machines perceive and interact with their environment. The thread of our exploration stitched through complex scenarios in robotics, detailed the intricacies of computer vision, and unveiled the mechanics behind autonomous systems. Each chapter brought to light how spatial reasoning—when augmented by AI—transforms vast arrays of data into insightful, actionable knowledge that machines can use to make informed decisions.

The practical applications discussed—ranging from navigating drones, facilitating robotic surgeries, to enhancing virtual reality—illustrate the vast potential and real-world impact of integrating spatial intelligence with artificial intelligence. These examples have not only underscored the versatility of spatial AI but also highlighted the ongoing challenges and ethical considerations that accompany its implementation. It's evident that while spatial AI promises substantial benefits, it necessitates cautious governance and ethical frameworks to prevent misuse and ensure its benefits are equitably distributed.

Reflecting on the book's overall impact, it becomes clear that it serves as a beacon for both novices and professionals in the field. By breaking down complex theories and weaving them into tangible examples, the book invites readers to appreciate the nuanced interplay between human-like reasoning and machine precision.

As you set this book aside, ponder on the future trajectory of spatial intelligence within AI. Consider the ethical implications as AI continues to evolve and further integrates into various facets of life. Think about the roles you might play, whether as developers, policymakers, or informed citizens in shaping a future where AI and spatial intelligence coexist responsibly and beneficially.

In closing, this book is more than just a compendium of knowledge—it is a prompt for continuous learning and active participation in one of the most dynamic fields of our time. As spatial intelligence continues to shape our technological landscape, let this book be both a foundation and a springboard for your own exploration and contributions to the field.

ABOUT THE AUTHOR

Jon Adams brings a wealth of experience from over twenty years in the information technology industry, having worked with some of the world's leading tech giants. With a deep-seated passion for science, technology, and languages, Jon excels at demystifying complex subjects, making them accessible and engaging to a broad audience.

His writings focus on breaking down intricate topics into everyday terms, helping readers not just learn but also apply this knowledge in their daily lives.

Currently, Jon is a proud member of Green Mountain Publishing, which publishes his insightful books. Through his work, he aims to foster a deeper understanding and appreciation of technology and science, enriching readers' lives.

www.ingramcontent.com/pod-product-compliance
Lightning Source LLC
LaVergne TN
LVHW051241050326
832903LV00028B/2506